Endorsements

“This book is for any woman who feels weighed down by pain and is longing for freedom. It reads like sitting on the sofa with a trusted sister-friend—shoes off, bare-faced—talking about the real things women often carry in silence.

With raw honesty, Rosita shares her journey through betrayal, disappointment, and hidden pain, revealing how God met her in the middle of the mess and transformed her wounds into strength. By the final page, you will have cried, laughed, and exhaled—realizing you are not alone. These pages will help you see that freedom is within reach.” —**R. Williams**

“This is so much more than a book—it is a sacred turning point. Within these pages, Rosita offers women the permission many have been quietly waiting for: permission to release what no longer serves them, to rise from pain, and to move forward with courage and clarity.

With honesty, wisdom, and deep compassion, she walks beside the reader through the vulnerable space between who they have been and who they are becoming. If you find yourself standing at the threshold of change, wondering if it’s finally time to step into a new chapter, Rosita’s voice is exactly the one you want guiding you forward.” —**Gabrielle Logan**

“This book is for every woman who feels stuck...almost numb to their emotions because they’ve been tolerating unacceptable behavior for so long!! First of all, you are not alone!! You will learn through Rosita’s powerful journey how to “move” your soul from bondage into freedom!!” —**Joni Ferreira**

A Woman's Journey from Pain to Power

THAT'S IT!
I'M MOVING

ROSITA PEREZ

Published by She Rises Studios Publishing
www.SheRisesStudios.com.

ISBN: 978-1-971349-72-5

This book is a work of creative non-fiction and personal truth. Names and identifying details may be changed to protect privacy.

Dedication

To God

who has carried me through the toughest storms. Your love for me is unconditional. You have healed me, revealed my gifts, and reminded me of the worth I carry. I am forever grateful.

To my daughter

my only child, my baby girl. Our journey together has not always been easy, but my love for you has never wavered. You are deeply treasured, and no matter what, I will always love you with all my heart.

To my precious grandsons

Your love has been a light in my life, lifting me in ways you may never fully know. You have filled my days with laughter, joy, and purpose, reminding me what it means to be truly loved. You are my treasures, and I thank God every day for the gift of you both.

To Teresita, Dorez, Vince, and Mirjam

you lifted me when I cried, made me laugh in my pain, reminded me of the strength you saw in me, and prayed for me when I couldn't lift my own arms. Your love and encouragement have carried me through more than words can say.

With enduring love and overflowing gratitude,
I dedicate this book to you all.

From Survival to Freedom

A Personal Letter

If you're holding this book, something inside you likely resonates with the title.

That's It! I'm Moving.

Not necessarily from one house to another...
but from the emotional places many of us live in far longer than we should.

Over time, women can find themselves living inside invisible houses built from old beliefs, past wounds, survival patterns, and stories we began telling ourselves long ago.

At first, those houses feel familiar.
Sometimes they even feel safe.

But eventually something begins to stir.

And the life we're living no longer fits the woman we are becoming.

Somewhere deep inside, a realization begins to rise:

I can't keep living like this.

If that's you, I want you to know something first:

I see you.
And you are not the only woman who has ever felt this way.

This book is for every woman.

For the woman whose heart carries quiet questions.
For the woman holding wounds she rarely speaks about.
For the woman whose faith is strong — and the woman whose faith feels fragile, distant, or complicated.

And for the woman who appears fine on the outside while something inside whispers,

There has to be more than this.

My hope is that within these pages you begin to see your story more clearly — not with shame, but with understanding.

Because when a woman finally sees the patterns that shaped her, something powerful begins to happen.

She realizes she is not broken.

She has simply been surviving.

And survival, while necessary for a season, was never meant to be the place where your life stays.

You don't have to have everything figured out today.

You only need the courage to open the door.

And perhaps the moment you open this book is the moment something inside you quietly decides:

That's it... I'm moving.

Believe It ~ Speak It ~ BE It!
Rosita

My Story

For years, I was frozen in survival.
I was alive, but I wasn't truly living yet.

Life kept moving forward, yet something inside me remained the same — a quiet ache, a loneliness I couldn't quite name, and patterns I couldn't seem to break.

Underneath it all was loss.

Loss can take many forms — the loss of a parent, a marriage, a dream, or the life you once believed you would have. Sometimes it's the loss of safety. Sometimes it's the loss of who you thought you were.

Loss has a quiet way of whispering abandonment into the most vulnerable places of the heart. Over time, that whisper shaped my thoughts, my relationships, and the way I saw myself.

But somewhere in my fifties, something inside me began to shift.

Not with answers — just a deep knowing:

I can't stay here.

I didn't know exactly where I was going, but I began to trust the One who could guide me.

So I made a commitment to myself: to stop hiding, to face my story honestly, and to begin the courageous work of healing.

Through trauma therapy, honest reflection, and a deeper surrender to God, something remarkable began to happen.

Little by little, the weight lifted.

I didn't just heal.

I reclaimed the woman I had always been — the one buried beneath loss, fear, and survival.

She was still there.

Waiting.

This book traces that journey — not perfectly, not quickly, but honestly. Through loss, identity shifts, hidden wounds, and the sacred work of becoming free.

If you have ever felt stuck in patterns you can't explain...
carrying pain you rarely speak about...
or wondering why you keep ending up in the same emotional place...

You are not broken.
You are not behind.
And you are not alone.

From pain to power.
From surviving to thriving.
From stuck... to becoming.

And if something inside you is stirring as you read these words, perhaps this is your moment.

A moment to say for yourself:

That's it... I'm moving.

Your new chapter starts with one step.

Let's begin.

Table of Contents

INTRODUCTION

The First Step Toward Discovering the Woman You're Becoming

Before we go any further, take one slow breath.

Unclench your jaw.
Drop your shoulders.

Transformation doesn't begin with perfection.

It begins with honesty.

With the courage to look at your life and ask:

Does this still fit me?

For years, I didn't ask that question.

I thought my pain was random.
Disconnected seasons.
Unrelated detours.

Until I began to see the pattern.

The rooms.
The houses.
The moving.

They weren't just metaphors.

They were mirrors.

For decades, as a real estate agent, I've helped people move in and out of homes. I've watched them pause in doorways, quietly wrestling with the same question:

Do I stay with what's familiar...
or step into something that fits who I'm becoming?

I've seen women leave beautiful homes filled with tension and walk into spaces that, though unfamiliar, felt lighter, calmer, and more aligned with who they had grown into.

Every move begins the same way:

With a decision.

With a quiet truth:

This no longer feels like home.

Somewhere along the way, I realized I wasn't just helping people move houses.

I was learning how to move forward.

How to release what no longer fits.
How to choose peace over history.

What I practiced professionally, I began to live personally.

And what I've lived, I now share with you.

This book isn't just about houses, rooms, and doors.

It's about recognizing when it's time to move.

And offering the path I walked
so you can make it your own.

If something inside you is stirring as you read this...
that's not accidental.

That's courage waking up.
That's freedom beginning to move.

CHAPTER 1

Where Have I Been Living?

The Courage to See the Truth About My Life

As you read these pages, notice what stirs inside you.

If a sentence resonates, pause and write it down.

Often, the words that linger are the ones meant to guide us forward.

Because sometimes, in the quiet honesty of reflection,
a woman begins to notice something she can no longer ignore:

**"I've been living in rooms inside myself
I never meant to stay in —
and somehow, they have become home."**

Not a physical home —
an emotional one.

The place shaped by what we survived,
what we lost,
what we carried,
and what we never said out loud.

Most of us don't choose these inner addresses.
We arrive there slowly —
through heartbreak, responsibility, silence,
and years of tending to everyone else
while neglecting the parts of ourselves
that were aching for attention.

Chapter 1 isn't about blame.
It's about clarity.
It's about gently looking at the life behind your life —

the house you've been living in emotionally,
sometimes for years or even decades.

If we were sitting together right now,
I wouldn't offer you the polished version of my story.

I'd offer you the truthful one —
the one that reveals where I was actually living inside myself,
and why it took so long to see it.

Because the heart has rooms
we don't enter until we're ready.

Rooms we inherit.
Rooms we build.
Rooms we outgrow.
Rooms we stay in long after the lights have gone out.

Some women live in:

- Silence
- Crumbs
- Survival
- Pretending
- Compromise
- Conflict
- Co-dependence

Not because we failed —
but because life required more of us
than we ever had space to name.

This chapter is the beginning of that naming.

It's the moment I finally saw
the emotional houses that shaped my decisions,
my relationships,
my strength,
and my exhaustion.

It's where the truth surfaced
and whispered:

"Where you've been living
does not have to be where you stay."

Naming it
was my first doorway out.

Understanding Where I've Been Living

Seeing the Spaces My Pain Built

Before healing can ever take root,
there comes a moment —
quiet, unsettling, undeniable —
when a woman finally pauses long enough to whisper to herself:

"Where am I living right now?"

Not her mailing address —
her **emotional address.**

The place in her soul she has been inhabiting
without realizing it had become home.

When I finally asked myself that question,
something shocking surfaced:

I had been living in emotional houses
I never consciously chose —

and some I stayed in
far longer than my spirit could bear.

Life didn't ask permission
before moving me into them —

loss did,
duty did,
trauma did,
survival did.

And because I didn't have language
for where I was living emotionally,

I assumed it was normal,
or worse —
that it was all I deserved.

Sis... this is why clarity matters.

**We cannot leave a place
we refuse to name.**

So let me walk you through
the houses I lived in —

not to overwhelm you,
but to **light a lantern**
so that maybe you can recognize yours too.

Because healing doesn't begin
with change —
it begins with **awareness.**

And as you read these next pages,
you may feel the gentle sting of recognition —
not because our stories are identical,
but because many daughters were raised
in the same emotional architecture.

Together,
let's walk through the rooms we have lived in,
so we can finally learn
how to walk out of them.

The House of Silence & Strength

It was a summer day.
My sister and I had just come home from riding bikes.
We walked through the door and saw our siblings sitting quietly—
faces sad, eyes lowered,
as if the air itself was holding bad news.

Then the phone rang.
It was my father.

And when he wailed the words, crying,
“She’s gone,”
something inside me went numb and blank.

I don’t remember much after that—
my body went on autopilot,
my emotions shut down just to survive.

Rosaries, the burial,
a house full of people
and then suddenly,
an empty one.

After my father said the words “She’s gone,”
life didn’t pause so we could grieve our mom—
it simply shifted beneath us.

There were no conversations about loss,
no space to unravel,
no language for heartbreak.

We were all in shock—
each of us carrying pain separately,
unsure how to hold our own grief,
let alone sit inside someone else’s.

What replaced mourning were tasks:

- Cook
- Clean
- Keep the house running
- Help the younger ones
- Make sure Dad could function
- Don’t fall apart
- Don’t need too much
- Don’t cry

Grief didn’t leave—
it just moved into the background,
quietly rearranging the rooms inside me.

After the funeral,
the house emptied—
but responsibility remained.

I was the oldest left at home,
and culturally, that meant one thing:
I step up—whether I am ready or not.

That was the day childhood ended—
not through time,
but through assignment.

I inherited a role
that wasn't spoken but deeply understood:
pseudo-adult, caretaker,
the strong one.

And strength
did not come from maturity—
it came from expectation.

My worth became measured in:

- what I could carry,
- how well I held everyone else together,
- how little I required.

Neighbors praised me:

"You're so responsible."
"So mature."
"Such a strong young woman."

I wore their words like armor—
because praise became
the only affection available.

On the outside,
I looked capable, composed, dependable—
the girl who could make everything work.

But inside?

I was a teenage girl,
standing in the kitchen after everyone went to bed,
washing the same plate twice—
because putting it down
might be the moment
I finally collapsed
into grief I didn't know how to express.

The unspoken rules of our house were clear:

- Be strong.
- Don't cry.
- Keep moving.
- The family needs you.
- Your feelings can wait.

This became my first emotional address:
The House of Silence & Strength.

A house where resilience was praised
but vulnerability was starved.
Where competence became identity,
and being needed replaced being nurtured.

For me, it began with loss —
the loss of my mother.
A grief too big for a little girl to carry.
An absence that quietly shaped everything.

But abandonment doesn't always begin with death.

Sometimes it begins with emotional distance.
With expectations placed too early.
With being the strong one before you were ever held.

Maybe your story looks different than mine.

Maybe no one left.
Maybe everyone stayed.

And still... something in you learned
not to need too much.
Not to feel too deeply.
Not to ask to be comforted.

Maybe you've lived there too —
where the world admires
how well you hold it all together,
but overlooks the girl inside you
who doesn't remember being held at all.

We didn't choose this house —
we were ushered into it
by loss, expectation,
and unacknowledged pain.

But naming the house
is not self-pity —
it is truth-telling.

And truth-telling
is the first crack in the walls.

Now you get to decide:

Will you stay in the house built by old pain —
or begin building one rooted in truth and freedom?

Because once you recognize the house,
you can finally see the door.

And seeing the door
is where the journey
from pain to power begins.

The House of Crumbs

Mistaking Attention for Love

Still in high school —
still carrying adult responsibilities on teenage shoulders —

I met a nineteen-year-old with a car, a swagger,
and a soft spot for me.

He drank too much.
But he also noticed me.

After losing my mom,
his attention felt like oxygen.

He called me beautiful.
He showed up.
He hugged me tight.

And in a house where my grief had no words
and my needs had no room,
his focus on me felt like love.

Until he cheated.

My heart broke loudly in my chest
but quietly in my world.
No one knew the depth of it.
I brushed it off, kept moving, and acted "fine."

Because by then
I had already learned to keep my pain quiet —
to push it deep down where no one could see it.

Then — one night —
he showed up at my door.
Drunk.
Crying.
Apologizing.
Promising change.
Begging me to take him back.

I stood behind the door,
my hand on the knob,

my heart was pounding.

A part of me wanted to let him in.
To feel chosen.
To not feel so alone.
To not lose the one person
who seemed to see me.

But something deeper —
something small and fierce inside me —
whispered:

No.
This isn't love.
This is not what you need.

I didn't open the door.

And though I didn't recognize it then,
that moment became my first act of self-respect.
The first time I chose
to feed my soul instead of my loneliness.

Later, I realized the truth behind what was happening:

I had been living in **The House of Crumbs** —
calling attention "love,"
accepting whatever I could get
because I didn't yet believe I deserved more.

And because I never learned how to process my pain,
I learned to accept crumbs silently —
hoping they would fill an emptiness
I wasn't allowed to name.

But here's what I wish someone had told me back then —
and what I want to tell you now:

- I wasn't broken — I was grieving.
- I wasn't needy — I was longing to be nurtured.
- I wasn't weak — I was carrying more than I was ever meant to carry alone.

I didn't understand it then —
but science now validates what my life lived.

A 2024 study titled **Losing a Parent During Childhood: The Impact on Adult Romantic Relationships** (van Heijningen et al.) found that early parental loss dramatically increases the struggle to build secure relationships later in life.

Not because we are damaged beyond repair —
but because when nurturing disappears too soon,
the nervous system learns to grip anything that feels like a connection.

So if you ever stayed too long,
tolerated too much,
or convinced yourself crumbs were enough —

Sis... science says it wasn't because you lacked strength.
It was because your heart was trying to survive
a wound it never got to name.

With the mindset of a sixteen-year-old,
I unknowingly did something quietly brave:
I chose differently.

And even though I didn't fully understand it yet,
something small but powerful
shifted inside me.

The House Of Survival

Love, Awakening, and My Daughter

At nineteen, I fell in love with a man who wrote me poetry and made promises that sounded like they could erase the ache I carried. The idea of a forever, a partner—it felt like hope.

We met and married within the same year.
One month later, I found out I was pregnant.

Our baby girl arrived in late 1981 —
tiny fingers, healthy weight, soft breathing —

a child made from love,
my greatest gift from above.

When they placed her on my chest, time stopped.
This is forever, I thought.
This is what love is supposed to feel like.

And for a little while,
I let myself believe the story I had always wanted to live.

But slowly — in tiny ways I didn't yet recognize as signs —
the cracks began to show.

Little comments that made me doubt my memory.

Blame that twisted every problem into my fault.

Emotional blows that slipped beneath the radar
because I needed the picture to work —
and I was invested in the story.

Then, in 1982, the physical abuse began.
And it didn't stop.

For a while, I held onto the hope of

the family I had imagined —
the security I craved,
the stability I desperately needed.

I kept believing it could still become what I longed for.

But there comes a moment
when a woman can't pretend anymore.

And for me, that moment had a name —
my baby girl.

I did not want her

- to grow up believing abuse was "normal" —
- tiny eyes watching me shrink,
- little heart learning that love meant fear, or silence,

- to learn how to cover wounds hidden beneath clothes.

I want her to know safety.

I want her to know peace.

I want her to see a mother who stood up,
not a mother who stayed down.

Because she did not deserve to grow up in abuse.

And the truth is — the world I was living in
made that choice even heavier.

In the early 1980s, experts estimated that domestic violence affected 1 in 10 marriages —
yet fewer than 10% of incidents were ever reported.
(*U.S. Senate Hearing on Domestic Violence, 1980; National Family Violence Surveys 1980–1985*)

Back then, abuse lived in the shadows.

Women were told to keep quiet,
to "work it out,"
to protect the family image,
to endure what was happening behind closed doors.

Leaving wasn't seen as strength —
it was whispered about as failure.

The shame was suffocating.
The fear was paralyzing.

And mothers carried all of it —
the bruises, the secrets, the blame —
while doing everything they could
to shield their children from the storm inside their homes.

But I knew something had to change.

I refused to let that become my daughter's memory of childhood —
or the legacy she would carry into her own life.

So I had to find the courage to leave.

At 22 —
with trusted friends steadying my courage —
I packed diapers and hope,
lifted my daughter onto my hip,
and walked out.

My daughter and I went back to my dad's house
to rebuild.

The divorce became legally final in 1985.
But my heart took much longer to heal.

I returned to what I learned at 15:

- Push it down.
- Keep going.
- Don't fall apart.
- Do what needs to be done.

Only now —
I have my little girl watching.

I was her security.
I had to be steady —
even when I was shaking inside.

Those years became **The House of Survival.**

By day, I worked hard to provide.
By night, I was a single mom.

I was determined to give my daughter opportunities
that would help her discover her gifts —
opportunities I wish I had experienced growing up.

I wanted her to grow up knowing she mattered —
that her voice was safe,
that she was seen.

What I didn't realize then
was that while I was trying to protect her future,
God was quietly protecting mine.

I wasn't saved yet.
I didn't know Jesus personally.

But even then —
before I had the language,
before I understood the theology —
HE was carrying me.

HE sent the right people.
HE opened the right doors.
HE placed strength inside me
that I did not naturally have.

Something greater than me
was already at work.

Survival became my shelter.
And thank God for shelters.

But shelters are not meant to be
permanent addresses.

If we stay too long in survival,
we tend to forget what it feels like
to breathe deeply,
to receive support,
to desire more than just "making it."

What I didn't know then
but can see clearly now — is this:

Survival trains you to function,
but it doesn't teach you to heal.

Survival gives you strength,
but it doesn't give you wholeness.

Survival protected us —
but eventually,
it began to confine me.

Survival served me —
until it began to cost me.

Healing Beyond Survival

For years, I carried the weight of what he had done —
the anger, the memories, and the questions that had no answers.

Without realizing it, that pain followed me.
Into my thoughts.
Into my relationships.
Into the quiet places of my heart.

It was like living in a prison built from a past that was already over.

As the years passed and healing began to rewire the truth inside me, I realized God was leading me to forgive the man who had abused me.

Not because what he did was acceptable.
Not because the years of pain suddenly disappeared.

But because God was inviting me into freedom, I didn't even realize I was missing.

So I learned how to forgive my daughter's father.

Over time, I came to understand something I could never have seen back then:

My forgiveness wasn't about excusing him.
My forgiveness didn't free him.
It freed me.

When I forgave, the chains didn't fall off him.
They fell off me.

Forgiveness didn't rewrite what happened.
It didn't pretend the wounds weren't real.

But it did something powerful.

It unlocked the door that had kept me standing in a house of pain I no longer had to live in.

Sometimes the first real step toward freedom is realizing you're allowed to walk out and leave that house behind.

Not quickly.
Not to appear noble.
Not to excuse what happened.

But because clarity revealed the deeper reality beneath our story.

I began to see that we were two wounded children wearing adult bodies — drawn to each other through our deficiencies, our unmet needs, and the ache neither of us had ever been taught to name.

I believe we both carried good intentions — to build a home, a family, a life that worked.

But our childhood wounds won that battle long before either of us knew how to fight differently.

Years later — after our daughter had grown into an adult and the wounds had scarred over — my wasbund asked me for forgiveness.

I never expected to hear those words.

It didn't erase the past, but it unhooked the shame.

That moment allowed something in me to heal even deeper.

It softened the edges and began to close the chapter with compassion instead of bitterness.

Forgiveness didn't change what happened.

But it opened the door to freedom.

And sometimes the bravest step a woman can take
is walking out of the house of pain
and choosing not to live there anymore.

Sis... if anything in my story touches a place in you that feels unsafe, you don't have to face that alone.

If you are in an unsafe situation,
or unsure whether what you are experiencing is abuse,
please reach out:

National Domestic Violence Hotline (U.S.)
1-800-799-SAFE (7233)
Text: **START** to 88788
www.thehotline.org

You are not alone.
You deserve safety — always.

You deserve to be heard.
You deserve to be treated with dignity and compassion.

The Houses of Pretending & Compromise

Wearing the 1980s Superwoman cape

The '80s told women we could do it all and have it all— even if we are divorced, and so many of us tried.

Career woman.
Mom.
Provider.
Helper.
Fixer.
Peacemaker.
College Student

Everything.

The message was loud and shiny:
Women can do it all.

And in some ways, it seemed to be true.
More doors were opening —
more jobs,

more independence,
more awareness around abuse,
more ways out.

But there was also the part no one talked about:

The stigma.
The shame.
The loneliness.
The pressure.

Being a divorced, single parent came with quiet judgments — some spoken, many unspoken.

It meant carrying the responsibility of raising a child while navigating my own healing.

It meant learning how to be both strong and tender at the same time.

There were days I wondered if I had failed.
Days I questioned whether I would ever feel whole again.

But somewhere in that season, something deeper was forming.

Strength.
Faith.
And a determination to rebuild a life that was not defined by what had broken me.

Because being a single mother wasn't the end of my story.

It was the beginning of discovering who I truly was.

So, I put on the Superwoman cape.

By day, I was a capable professional.
By night, a single mom —
making dinner, helping with homework, paying the bills,
holding everything together,
and quietly hoping I was enough.

Some days I felt strong, and other days I wondered if I was holding everything together by a thread.

On the outside, I was roaring with strength —
unstoppable.

On the inside?

I was deeply tired,
and deeply searching —

- for a love that would stay,
- for a place to set the burden down,
- for someone who would finally see me.

And beneath that search lived a wound I didn't yet have language for:

I was angry.
Still grieving the abandonment I carried from losing my mom.

Longing for love —
while pushing it away at the same time
because another loss felt unbearable.

My heart wanted stability.
My nervous system expected loss.
And living in that contradiction
is its own kind of exhaustion.

Still, I entered two long-term relationships.

They had their beautiful parts —
inside jokes, shared memories, holidays, road trips,
the "us" moments that made the picture look right.

I truly felt love —
and I believed it was mutual —
but only through the limited understanding
our wounded hearts could offer each other.

I wasn't unhappy — I was unknowing.

What I didn't know at the time is this:
Unhealed people often find each other —
not out of romance, but out of recognition.

Looking back with compassion —
for myself and for them —
I can see what I couldn't see then:

We weren't drawn together because we were whole.
We were drawn together because our wounds were familiar.

Their emotional distance matched my abandonment wound.

My over-functioning matched their under-giving.

My strength paired with their need for rescue.

Their inconsistency mirrored the loss I had never processed.

It wasn't love pulling us together —
it was deficiency searching for deficiency.

Pain reaching toward what feels familiar.
Loneliness seeking companionship —
even when that companionship is unsteady.

And Sis… that isn't crazy.

It's human
when we're carrying emotional baggage
we were never taught how to unpack.

Attachment researchers Mikulincer and Shaver explain that early caregiving experiences can shape how adults experience closeness, trust, emotional regulation, and conflict in romantic relationships.

For many women, this can quietly show up in patterns such as:

- fearing abandonment
- struggling to trust love when it is offered
- becoming highly sensitive to signs of distance or withdrawal

- over-functioning to keep the relationship stable
- tolerating emotional imbalance
- staying longer than their peace was asking them to

Sometimes what we judge ourselves for is simply the echo of wounds that were never given the chance to heal.

Not because we are weak —
but because our hearts learned
that love and loss often arrive together.

So underneath it all,
I kept adjusting myself to fit.

Not by talking softer —
because I've never been a quiet woman —
but by lowering my expectations,
convincing myself I didn't need much.

I tried to need less.
Tried to want less.
Tried to make peace with crumbs.

I over-functioned —
giving more than I received,
carrying more than was mine to carry,
hoping that effort could somehow bridge the emotional distance.

And emotionally,
I swung between wanting more
and being angry that I wasn't getting it —

then retreating into passive-aggressive silence
because I didn't know how to close the gap
between longing and self-protection.

I wasn't apologizing for my needs.
I was wrestling with them.

Punishing myself for having them.
Resenting him for not meeting them.

Pretending I was fine
when I was anything but.

It was a vicious, crazy-making cycle —
one that can only be broken through healing.

As you read this, you may be recognizing pieces of your own story.

Have you ever punished yourself for needing more — while quietly resenting someone for leaving those needs unmet?

If so, please hear this:
recognizing the pattern is not failure —
it's the beginning of freedom.

I didn't have that language then.
All I knew was that something inside me
was growing tired of the same pain.

Near the end of each relationship,
in the quiet moments when I finally stopped performing strength,
I had to admit the truth:

The chaos, fighting, and constant tension were stripping my peace, and my body, mind, and spirit had reached their limit.

The breakups felt like déjà vu —
heartbreak on repeat.

Looking back,
I can finally name what I couldn't see then:

These were the years I lived
in **The House of Pretending and Compromise.**

Smiling for photos
while the foundation of my life was quietly cracking.

Staying because "not being alone"
felt safer
than admitting
I still felt empty.

And during that time,
all the *selfs* grew loud:

self-doubt
self-blame
self-criticism
self-neglect
self-rejection
self-sabotage

I was exhausted from holding up a life
that wasn't holding me.

And those years taught me
one of the hardest truths a woman in midlife can face:

Pretending is expensive.
Compromise can cost your soul.

Because behind every woman who stayed too long,
there is a story.

And it often looks something like this:

Women who...

- grew up too fast
- carried a family before they carried themselves
- lost a parent and never had time to heal
- survived abuse and rebuilt life from the ashes
- raised children alone
- chased love they didn't receive
- stayed longer than their heart wanted
- tried — with everything in them — to make it work

We didn't lose ourselves because we were weak.

We lost ourselves because we were trying to love
with wounds that were never given time to heal.

And now?

Sis... now we have a choice.

We can keep carrying the story —
or we can finally begin telling the truth.

The House of Conflict & Co-Dependence

Ignoring the Whisper and Calling It Love

By the time I reached my mid-thirties, something in me was changing.

After years of being strong, holding up relationships that couldn't hold me back, and trying to outwork my wounds, something inside me began to shift.

I was tired of the chaos.
Tired of surviving.

I wanted to rest.
I needed to heal.

And before I fully understood why, I found myself standing at a different kind of doorway.

A local Christian church.

As worship began, it softened something in me that had been brittle for years.

Emotions surfaced that I had kept buried for decades.

Tears came — not loud, but honest —
the kind that slips out
when your soul finally grows quiet enough to be heard.

And then, for the first time in my life,
I felt a presence —
a peace so quiet
and a love so gentle
it stilled everything inside me.

And in that stillness, I began to feel myself again —
nurturing the parts of me I had abandoned
while trying to keep life from falling apart.

As life began to move forward again,
I met a man who said he loved God, too.

He was kind.
He was charming.
He believed.
And something in me exhaled.

I thought, *Maybe this is it.*
Maybe this is my "forever after."

Looking back, I probably wasn't ready.
And once again, I slowly stopped tending to myself
and began centering my life around a man.

Have you ever done that?

So hopeful for love
that you start neglecting the very parts of yourself
that need care the most?

We dated for two years.

Driven by the heartbreak of relationships before him,
I eventually gave an ultimatum:

"Commit or quit."

And weeks before the wedding,
there were signs —
and deep in my spirit, I felt a clear **no**.

Not a warning drenched in fear —
a quiet caution wrapped in love.

I heard it.
But I pushed past it.

I asked, *Lord, why not?*

He's a Christian.
He says he loves me.
He seems like everything I've been wanting.

Why would I walk away from this?

So I didn't.

Later that year, we were married.

We tried to build a blended family—
something neither of us had healthy examples for
and no real roadmap to follow.

Still, we created memories:

Birthday parties.
Graduations.
Holidays.
Family laughter.
Shared loss.

There was love.
There was history.
More than a decade of investment.

And because of that investment,
it was easy to wear blinders
to the parts of our marriage that weren't healthy—

- lack of partnership
- lack of respect
- lack of transparency

But around year fourteen,
the threads began to unravel.

Finances exposed the fault lines.

I came to the table with solutions—
cutting budgets, shifting expenses,
reducing housing costs so we could breathe again
and protect what we had built.

But it was a one-way street.

Somewhere along the way,
control had taken root
where partnership was meant to grow.

And in that moment, I realized something
I had never been taught to see.

I had slowly surrendered my voice.

Not because I was weak,
but because I truly believed at the time
that being a "good wife" meant carrying the weight quietly
while letting him lead completely.

What I didn't truly understand then
is that a healthy marriage is built on partnership —

two people sharing responsibility,
sharing truth,
and honoring each other's voice
as equal and essential.

But the imbalance had been sealed for years.

And when only one person is steering,
there is no way to turn things around.

I felt confined.
Trapped.

Slowly losing pieces of myself.

Debt deepened.
Stress tightened.
Arguments sharpened.

Silence grew louder than any conversation we tried to have.

We pulled away
instead of drawing close.

I felt disrespected.
Unheard.
Unseen.
Unvalued.

Old wounds lit up like a switchboard.

Hurt.
Sadness.
Anger.
Resentment.
Defeat.

We stopped praying together.
We stopped partnering.
We stopped being *us*.

I moved into another room.

And we became roommates with rings.

I kept praying —
though looking back,
my prayers were more about what I hoped for
than what God wanted for our marriage.

Then one night,
after painful fighting words were hurled at me,
every part of me wanted to react —
to match hurt for hurt,
fire for fire.

But God.

My body went still.
My tongue froze.

It was as if heaven placed
divine brakes on my anger.

And in that stillness,
I saw a vision:

Me behind the plexiglass,
explaining to my grandson
why Nana was in jail.

That broke my heart.

That moment of mercy
stopped a consequence
I could never undo.

And it saved my future.

The next day,
I moved out.

We separated for a year and a half
and "worked on the marriage."

I believed the promises made
and moved back home.

Within months,
promises were broken again.

My health declined.
My spirit dimmed.

The ground crumbled beneath us.

And still...

I stayed for another five years.

During that time,
I drew closer to God —
and God drew closer to me.

But the marriage remained fractured.

You see, no matter how much one person grows,
a marriage still requires two hearts
committed to each other
and moving toward healing and restoration.

Then one night,
I heard God whisper clearly in my spirit:

"Enough!
Neither one of you is glorifying Me in this marriage."

Two weeks later,
my husband —
now my *wasband* —
asked me to move out.

Twenty-one years.

Children raised.
Grandsons loved.
Family losses grieved.
Memories stacked.

Sis... through it all, I truly believed
we would be each other's forever after.

That week,
I packed, I cried
and I prayed.

I walked through rooms
that felt like museum exhibits of our life —
frozen, familiar, and quietly heartbreaking.

Truthfully,
those last five years had already revealed
what I didn't want to admit:

The marriage had become toxic.
The pain had become unbearable.

Every old wound screamed:

- You're not enough.
- You're unloved.
- You're unseen.
- You're alone.

And in my mind,
the same question circled again and again:

Should I stay?

Or should I go?

I was in the fight of my life.
And I knew either choice would hurt.

If I stayed,
our behavior was not honoring God.

Staying meant continuing a cycle
that was eroding my health,
dimming my spirit,
and asking me to silence myself
in the name of peace —
but there was no peace.

And truthfully,
time had already shown me
nothing was going to change.

If I left,
I would step into uncertainty —
financially, emotionally, spiritually.

No guarantees.
No map.
Just faith.

So I prayed for God's will, not mine.

I kept packing.

My *wasband* said the same words
he had said before:

"I'm sorry.
Don't go.
Stay."

But there were no new solutions.
No repair.
No hope.

Then the words rose in me —
clearer than my fear.

And I said them out loud:

"I love you.
And I love me too.

I have to leave because
this is the worst it's ever been."

And this time...

I chose to listen to God.

We separated again
and agreed to try rebuilding our marriage.

But leaving —
choosing myself
and trusting God —
was the most painful choice
I have ever made.

For the first time in my life,
I did not abandon myself
to keep a relationship.

It was unknown.
It was terrifying.

And I stepped forward,
not realizing
that moment would become the doorway
to the next house of my life.

A doorway I never imagined
would lead to freedom.

So at 57 years old,
I finally faced the truth:

I had been living
in the **House of Conflict & Co-dependence** —
and it had nearly swallowed me alive,
one quiet compromise at a time.

And if I stayed,
I knew I would lose myself completely.

That realization stopped me.

It pulled me inward —
back to a truth I had been too exhausted to face.

Sis...
when I finally stepped back far enough,
I could see the patterns shaping my life —

the rooms I hid in,
the walls I built,
the ceilings I lowered.

And something shifted.

Awareness didn't shame me.
It freed me.

It whispered:
You don't have to stay here.

And in that moment, I understood:

"I am not defined by the houses I lived in —
I am defined by the courage it takes to leave them."
— Rosita Perez

That's where my change began —

with honesty,
with compassion,

and with the courage
to walk toward a new address.

Being Honest & Accountable With Self

Facing The Truth With Courage, Not Shame

Sis...

The hardest person to be honest with
wasn't my wasbund.
It wasn't my family.
It wasn't even God.

It was me.

For years, I wore the masks:

"I'm fine."
"I've got it under control."
"I can handle it."

I showed up strong at work.
Strong at home.
Strong for everyone else —
even when I was breaking inside.

If strength had a face,
I wore the latest version.

But slowly, another truth began to surface —
one I hadn't wanted to face.

Strength without honesty
is exhaustion in disguise.

And for the first time,
I began to see
how deeply
I had been abandoning myself.

For decades I had been living in emotional rooms
I never consciously chose —

Silence.
Survival.
Pretending.
Compromise.
Conflict.

Rooms I learned to adapt to
in order to survive.

And then one day
something inside me grew still.

Not because life became quiet —
it didn't.

But inside me,
the running stopped.

No performing.
No fixing.
No bracing.

Just a pause.

And in that stillness
I finally knew the truth:

I can't keep doing this to myself.

That moment didn't accuse me.
It simply made space.

And in that space,
honesty could finally breathe.

Not the kind that shames —
the kind that gently asks:

What is true right now?

I knew I couldn't do this alone.

I had tried for decades —
and in many ways,
only delayed my own healing.

So, I asked for help.
I turned to God for guidance and strength. I did Eye Movement Desensitization and Reprocessing (EMDR)
--a therapy that helps heal painful memories—attended healing rooms and leaned on the support of my community.
Through these, I gained strength and began replacing the lies with truth.

Truth looked like this: the woman I thought I had lost... was a shell of who I am becoming.

I began to see that the lies I believed—that I wasn't enough, that I had to earn love, that my voice didn't matter—these were never mine to carry.

My truth is this: I am worthy, I am chosen, and my voice has always had value.

And with that truth... came the courage to face what I had been avoiding.

Admitting what hurt.
Naming what felt heavy.
Acknowledging what I had been tolerating
instead of choosing.

Admitting what hurt.
Naming what felt heavy.
Acknowledging what I had been tolerating
instead of choosing.

I stopped minimizing.
Stopped explaining it away.
Stopped pretending I was okay
when I wasn't.

This was the beginning —
not of answers,
but of awareness.

And awareness
is where every real turning point begins.

The Quiet Moment That Became My Turning Point

My turning point didn't arrive in a crisis.
There was no argument.
No dramatic moments.

It came on an ordinary afternoon —
the kind that looks small
until it quietly changes everything.

That was the afternoon
I finally allowed myself to be honest.

For years, I had been surviving —
pushing through,
holding everything together,
pretending I was stronger than I felt.

But in that quiet moment,
something deeper surfaced.

Not loud.
Not accusing.
Just clear.

And then a question rose from deep within:

Where are you really living right now?

Not my address.
Not my marriage.
Not the image I showed the world.

But emotionally.
Spiritually.
Mentally.

And for the first time,
I let myself look honestly.

The woman the world saw
was not the woman
living inside my heart.

That moment became my mirror —
not reflecting my face,
but revealing my truth.

**"You will know the truth,
and the truth will set you free."
—John 8:32**

And Sis...

that mirror was both
merciful
and honest.

What I didn't realize then
was that this quiet moment
had opened a door.

And on the other side of that door...
a truth was waiting for me.

Uncovering the Truth That Changed Everything

Once I allowed myself to look honestly,
something began to shift.

The truth was this:
I wasn't healing.
I was reliving the pain
again and again.

A quiet awareness began to surface.

Not all at once.
Not loudly.
Just a gentle noticing.

I began to see how often
I replayed the same painful stories in my mind,
hoping they would finally make sense.

But they never did.

They only deepened the wound.

That wasn't healing.

It was rumination —
a loop that kept me tied to rooms
I desperately wanted to leave.

Later, I learned what my heart
had already begun to uncover:

Rumination keeps the mind stuck in survival mode.
Instead of processing pain,
We rehearsed it.
Again and again.

No wonder I felt exhausted.
No wonder I felt stuck.

Because the truth was becoming clearer:

I couldn't move forward
until I stopped hiding from myself.

Now Sis... let me say this honestly.

I was afraid to look at my own life.
Afraid to unpack what had kept me stuck.

Every time I tried,
the old versions of me rushed back in —
the frightened one,

the fixer,
the performer,
the woman who survived by staying small.

For decades,
fear kept me circling the same patterns.

But this time
I refused to face it alone.

I called on my higher power —
and for me, that power is Jesus.

I needed Him to guide me,
to steady me
when the truth felt tender
and fear tried to pull me back.

Awakening didn't happen all at once.

But a door cracked open.

And through that opening,
God began placing three gentle keys in my hands.

Not heavy teachings.
Not overwhelming lessons.

Just small invitations
to step toward myself again.

These became
The Three Keys to My Breakthrough —

keys that would eventually open
every locked room
I thought I could never escape.

🔑 KEY 1 — TRUTH

The moment I stopped performing and started seeing

My truth didn't shout.
It whispered:

**"You can't heal
what you won't face."**

Truth became a mirror, not a hammer —
the moment I finally admitted,

"I'm not okay...
and it's time to understand why."

**I began paying attention to what I was truly feeling
instead of pretending everything was fine.
Little by little,
I allowed myself to be honest.**

🔍 KEY 2 — OWNERSHIP

The moment I realized I wasn't powerless

Ownership didn't come to condemn me.
It woke me up.

"I may not have caused all my pain,
but I have the power to choose
how long will I stay in it."

Ownership isn't blame.
It's power —
the power to choose differently.

**I began noticing the choices I was making
and the patterns I was repeating.
Little by little,
I started choosing differently.**

🔍 KEY 3 — BOUNDARIES

The moment I realized my needs mattered too

I didn't grow up understanding boundaries.
Life had to teach me —
through pain and through healing.

I began to understand that protecting my peace
is protecting my purpose.

And that real love
never asks me to disappear.

Boundaries didn't make me hard.
They made me clear.

And for the first time,
I knew I could love others
without losing myself.

I began paying attention to what brought peace into my life
and what quietly stole it away.
And little by little,
I began choosing differently.

These three keys didn't change everything overnight...

But they opened the door.

Truth helped me see myself.
Ownership helped me choose myself.
Boundaries helped me protect myself.

And slowly — gently —
I began finding my way back
to the woman God intended me to be.

I didn't master any of this right away.
I simply held on —
one truth, one choice, one boundary at a time.

Sis... I share this not because my path is *the* path,
but because naming what steadied me
helped me stop running from myself.

From that moment forward,
I was no longer walking into my healing
empty-handed.

Now... take a breath.

Look at the ground we've already covered.

We walked back through the rooms I survived —

Silence.
Crumbs.
Survival.
Pretending.
Compromise.
Conflict.

Not to relive them,
but to reclaim myself from them.

I looked honestly at where I had been living on the inside.

And that alone
is transformational work.

Remember:

Awareness doesn't judge you —
it frees you.

Because the moment we name where we are,
we open the doorway
to where we can go next.

So let me ask you, Sis...

Did anything in this chapter resonate with you?

Did a moment, a sentence, or a memory
quietly whisper, *"That's me."*

If it did, pause with that.

Reflection like this
is where courage begins.

And if you were willing to look honestly
at your own life while reading these pages,

I want you to know something:

I am proud of you.

Because you've taken a brave step —
not by finishing a chapter,
but by allowing yourself
to see something honestly.

And that kind of honesty
is where real change begins.

Reflect & Renew

Standing in My Truth

1. Pause & Reflect
Place one hand over your heart.
Take one slow breath.

Ask yourself gently:
"What house am I living in right now?"

Write one honest sentence.

Nothing polished. Nothing performative.

Just truth.

2. Truth to Hold
"I cannot heal what I refuse to name."
— Rosita Perez

Reflection:
What truth am I ready to name today?

3. One Small Step
Choose one:

- Speak one honest truth to yourself.
- Sit in stillness for three minutes.

Write down whatever came to mind.

Small steps lead to powerful change.

4. An Encouraging Word
Sis... you did meaningful work today.
You are not defined by where you've been.
You are defined by the courage rising inside you.

Speak one encouraging word over yourself — strong, worthy, brave, healing.

Pause for a moment and honor the courage it took to show up for yourself today.

CHAPTER 2

What Keeps Me Living Here?

Uncovering the Hidden Ties

I began to see that I hadn't stayed stuck for no reason.

Hidden ties were holding me there:

- childhood scripts I inherited without choosing
- pain I never gave myself permission to grieve
- responsibilities placed on me too soon
- patterns that once protected me but later confined me
- fears that whispered louder than faith
- familiarity that felt safer than freedom
- attachments I didn't realize were still holding me

Whew, this part of my journey was tender—
and sometimes frightening.

I knew I could not do it alone.

So I deepened my faith,
leaned into community,
worked with a therapist,
and surrounded myself with prayer warriors
who steadied me when the work felt heavy.

If this next step feels tender for you, too—
even a little scary—
I understand.

Go at your own pace.
Choose the support that feels right for you.

And if parts of my story sound familiar to you,
that's not an accident.

Sis...
take my hand.

Let's step in together.

Am I Living in My Childhood Home?

When Old Rooms Still Shape My Reality

"Am I still living in my childhood home?"

Not physically.
But emotionally.
Spiritually.
Mentally.

When I finally slowed down long enough to look inward,
I realized something I did not expect:

My body had grown up,
but part of my heart was still responding to life
like the little girl inside me.

The girl who felt unseen.
Who learned to stay strong.
Who became responsible because she had no choice.
Who learned that being needed
was the same as being loved.

Without even realizing it,
those early lessons became the blueprint
I was still living by.

We tell ourselves,
"That was years ago. I'm over it."

But if we look closer—really look—
many of us are still living by childhood rules
we never meant to carry:

- Don't cry
- Be strong
- Don't need anything from anyone
- Keep the peace
- Never be the problem
- Make everyone else happy
- Carry everything quietly
- Make everyone else comfortable

And Sis... you are not alone.

Research shows that **70% of women describe themselves as emotionally responsible for everyone around them — not because they want to be, but because they were taught to be.**

Those rules can follow us into adulthood
until the blueprint begins to suffocate us.

For me, therapy became one of the places
where God began untangling the roots.

My counselor did not break me open.
She simply held the space
I had never been given before.

Layer by layer.
Truth by truth.
Root by root.
The deeper truth surfaced:

- the grief of losing my mother at fifteen
- responsibility placed on my shoulders too early
- the loneliness hidden beneath "being strong"
- the anger of never being allowed to break
- the little girl who learned to survive, not to feel

And I began to see something clearly:

I was not strong because I had healed.
I was strong because I had learned to survive.

And chapter by chapter,
layer by layer,
I began walking out
of the house
that had shaped my reality.

What Keeps Me Tied Here?

Naming the Fears, Familiarities, and Ties That Keep Me Stuck

The hardest truth to admit was this:

Even after I realized I was stuck,
I stayed.

Why?

Because pain — even painful pain — can feel safer than the unknown.

Even when a room is suffocating,
it can still feel like home.
Not because it's healthy,
but because it's known.

I learned this the hard way.

There were seasons when I knew the relationship was over.
I knew the environment was draining me.
I knew the story was no longer serving me.

And yet... I stayed.

When I finally slowed down long enough to hear my own heart,
I realized something both painful and freeing:

I wasn't just living in an emotional house —
I was being held there by invisible ties.

Ties made of old beliefs.
Old wounds.
Old vows.

Old habits that once protected me
but now kept me small.

These ties didn't show up as drama.

They showed up as patterns.
As reactions.
As moments when I responded like the woman I used to be —
not the woman I was becoming.

And the truth became clear:

I wasn't stuck on purpose.

I was stuck because the familiar felt safer than the unknown.

Because here's what we rarely talk about:

Our brains are wired for familiarity — not freedom.

So we stay where things feel predictable:

- the pain is predictable
- the chaos feels normal
- the disappointment feels familiar
- the old story feels safer than writing a new one
- the unknown feels terrifying

That is not a weakness.

That is wiring.

And Sis... this matters:

Even unhealthy rooms can feel safer
than rooms we've never walked into.

**Because familiarity doesn't equal belonging —
It simply means you learned how to survive there.**

That's why leaving isn't just about packing emotional bags.

It takes something deeper.

It requires loosening the ties that once protected you
but now keep you stuck.

A woman doesn't remain in what's unhealthy without reason. Something beneath the surface is holding her there—fear, vows, patterns, or pain.

We don't always recognize them as ties.
But that's exactly what they are —
invisible threads pulling on your choices,
your confidence,
your sense of worth.

And this is where the real work begins.

The Psychological Ties We Don't See

I once read that most people repeat emotional patterns
not because they choose them —
but because the brain associates them with survival.

That truth pierced me.

Because the chaos I lived in had become familiar.

I knew how to

- brace for disappointment.
- navigate conflict.
- hold everyone else together while quietly falling apart.

But peace?
Joy?
Rest?
Being truly seen?

Those felt like foreign languages
I didn't yet know how to speak.

We stay tied because .....

- the pain is familiar.
- uncertainty feels dangerous.
- the nervous system confuses survival with love.

And Sis... hear this with your whole heart:

You did not choose these ties.

They formed quietly
as you did what you had to do to survive.

But now that you can see them,
you do not have to keep living under them.

**"Even the strongest women stay stuck
when the ties of old pain
are still wrapped around their hearts."
— Rosita Perez**

Leaving isn't just courage.

It is rewiring your emotional blueprint.

And before I could move forward,
I had to do something most of us avoid.

I had to name the ties.

The Ties Formed in Survival

Some ties were woven in childhood —
rules and roles I never meant to carry.

Others formed through heartbreak, trauma,
or seasons I never fully grieved.

And some came from the parts of me
that were simply trying to survive.

These were the ties I discovered in myself —
quiet, invisible threads
pulling on my choices and my life.

They might feel familiar to you, too.

Tie #1 — Unprocessed Anger

From losing my mother too young.
From an abusive marriage.
From carrying adult responsibilities
before my heart was ready.

I thought I buried it.

But buried pain doesn't disappear.
It echoes.

Sometimes it surfaced as impatience,
defensiveness, or a heart that
didn't know how to rest.

Tie #2 — Over-Responsibility

I learned early that being needed
made me valuable.

So I kept everyone else afloat —
even while I was drowning inside.

Over time, I stopped asking for help
because I believed everything
was mine to carry.

Tie #3 — Old Vows

Some promises were never spoken out loud —
but I lived by them.

"I'll handle it."
"I don't need anyone."
"I won't be a burden."

Those vows protected me as a girl.

But as a woman,
they kept me isolated —

wrapped in a protective pride
because accepting support
made me feel less than.

Tie #4 — The Fear of Letting Go

Letting go meant stepping into a future
I couldn't control myself.

And control had been my safety
for decades.

So I stayed longer than I should have —
in places that were slowly
draining the life out of me.

Tie #5 — A Mindset Shaped by Survival

I learned to live with a survivor's mindset —
always alert, always bracing.

So my mind wasn't open to ease
or the possibility of something better.

That mindset didn't just shape how I thought.

It shaped how I lived.

Every tie I carried was doing the same thing —
keeping me rooted in what I knew,
even when my soul was ready to move.

And the truth is...
many of the ties holding me there
were not mine alone.

Some were quietly passed down.
Some were learned by watching the women before me.
Some were shaped by expectations
about what a "good woman" should carry.

The more I looked around,
the more I realized:

**Many women are living with the same invisible ties —
silently carrying them
without ever naming them.**

Shared Ties: What Many Women Carry in Silence

Sis, some ties were in place long before you arrived.

Some are inherited.
Some are modeled.
Some are passed quietly through generations
of women who did the best they could
with what they had.

Others are shaped by culture —
by expectations placed on women
and messages repeated so often
they begin to feel like the truth.

These are shared ties —
the ones many women carry
without ever naming.

Familiar Pain

Sometimes the pain you grew up around
feels safer
than a life you've never seen lived.

"Good Girl" Conditioning

Be pleasant.
Be grateful.
Be quiet.
Be strong.

Don't cause problems.
Don't ask for too much.

Generations of women were taught
to disappear politely.

Emotional Loyalty

Staying because leaving feels disloyal —
to family,
to history,
to the woman who survived before you.

Somewhere along the way,
love became confused with endurance.

Carrying What Was Never Yours

Becoming the strong one.
The fixer.
The peacekeeper.

Holding emotional weight
that never belonged to you.

Survival Patterns

Over-functioning.
People-pleasing.
Self-silencing.
Shutting down to stay safe.

Patterns learned in homes,
churches,
relationships,
and reinforced by society.

Not because women are weak —
but because survival was required.

Take a minute, Sis, and ask yourself:

How many of these ties
have been quietly shaping your life?

Sis... pause here with me for a moment.

Take one slow breath.

What you've just uncovered
was never meant to condemn you —
it was meant to free you.

These ties do not define you.
They simply explain where you've been.

And now that you can see them,
they no longer have the same hold on you.

These ties were never meant
to be carried forever.

They were learned.
Passed down.
Inherited.

But they can end with you.

It's time to untie them.
To release what no longer belongs to your future.

So your heart can breathe again.

And so you, Sis, can become.

Choices I've Made

How My Choices Kept Me Here — and Set Me Free

Sis...

There came a day when I had to face one of the hardest truths of all:

No one was keeping me stuck but me.

Not intentionally.
Not consciously.
Not because I didn't want better —

but because I kept making choices
from old wounds, old fears,
and patterns I didn't yet realize
were running the show.

Every time I replayed my hurt...
Every time I stayed where I wasn't growing...
Every time I told my story
without allowing God to transform it...

I was choosing to remain
in the same emotional house.

Not because I loved it there.
But because it felt familiar.

**Sis... have you ever prayed for peace,
yet found yourself returning
to the chaos you knew?**

That was me.

I had grown so accustomed to what I now call **Victim Ville**
that I didn't even notice I had moved in.

Pain had a zip code.
Self-pity kept the lights on.
Blame decorated the walls.

And nothing — absolutely nothing — changed.

I didn't stay because I enjoyed the pain.
I stayed because part of me
didn't believe I could leave.

Then one morning,
standing in the mirror
with tired eyes and a tired heart,

I whispered,

“This cannot be my whole life.”

And in that quiet, trembling moment...

it felt as if heaven leaned close
and something inside me
finally began to shift.

I felt God whisper back:

“Daughter... you get to choose.”

That whisper didn’t erase my past.
It didn’t pretend the pain never happened.

But it reminded me of something
I had forgotten:

I still have the power
to choose my next chapter.

I didn’t have to know the whole plan.
I didn’t have to feel ready.
I didn’t have to fix everything overnight.

I only had to take one new step —
and trust that God would meet me there.

Because here is the truth
that finally set me free:

Every choice I make is a seed.
And I get to decide
what grows next.
— Rosita Perez

Once I understood that,
things began to change.

Not all at once.
Not dramatically.

But steadily...
quietly...
one brave decision at a time.

And looking back now,
I can see the moment
everything began to change.

The shift came down to two simple decisions.

Before we go deeper, Sis,
let me name them.

Choice One:
I stopped choosing what felt familiar —
even when familiar felt easier.

Choice Two:
I began choosing more carefully —
paying attention to patterns I had ignored before.

Those choices didn't fix everything.

But they changed where I stood.

And where you stand
determines where you can go next.

Those two decisions became the turning point
that moved me
from surviving my life
to becoming the woman
God created me to be.

Looking back, I can sum it up this way:

I stopped choosing what felt familiar.
I began choosing more carefully.

Come with me, Sis.
Let me show you how.

Choices That Shaped My Journey

Sis... you may recognize this pattern too.

The first place my choices showed up most clearly
was in my relationships.

Choice #1 — Staying in Unhealthy Relationships

Choosing What Felt Familiar

I stayed in relationships
that mirrored my unhealed places.

Every time I ignored red flags,
minimized dysfunction,
or told myself, *"It's not that bad,"*

I was choosing an emotional house
that slowly drained me.

Not because I wanted the pain —
but because familiar felt safer
than the unknown.

The cost of that choice:

- I lost pieces of myself.
- My confidence softened.
- My voice grew quiet.
- My joy dimmed.

Choosing More Carefully
Freedom didn't come through one dramatic exit.

It came through a quiet awakening.

I began paying attention
to patterns I had ignored before.

Little by little, my choices shifted:

Honesty over hope-that-hurts.
Healing over history.
My worth over my fear of being alone.

And with each small step,
I began finding my way back to myself.

Choice #2 — Leaving My Marriage

It took years before I realized
this same pattern had followed me
into my marriage.

Sis... you know my heart.

I believe deeply in marriage
and the sacred covenant it is meant to be.

Divorce was never the plan.
It was never an escape route.
It was the last, unwanted option.

And I also believe this:

A woman should never have to abandon herself
to be loved, honored, or chosen.

When we do,
we slowly become someone
we no longer recognize —
and that dishonors the woman God created us to be.

Choosing What Felt Familiar
For years, I stayed in a marriage
that was slowly breaking me.

I kept hoping things would change.
I kept praying harder.

But staying came at a cost.

- My peace disappeared.
- My health declined.
- My sense of self grew dim.

Not because I didn't believe in marriage —
but because leaving felt unimaginable.

<u>Choosing More Carefully</u>

Freedom didn't come through one dramatic decision.

It came through a painful awakening.

I began acknowledging
what my heart had been whispering for years.

Accepting that I could not change this alone.

Letting God meet me in my weakness —
and allowing the wisdom, support, and community
that gave me the courage
to step away from what was breaking me.

Leaving my marriage was not the choice I wanted.

It was the choice that saved my life.

"Leaving wasn't losing.
It was trusting God enough
to step away from what was breaking me."
— Rosita Perez

And I later realized

the step that broke my heart
was the very step
that began healing it.

Sis... sometimes the moment that breaks us open
is the one that finally sets us free.

What Finally Shifted — The Courage to Move Forward

This was not easy.

I was trembling, unsure, and afraid.

What changed wasn't confidence, clarity, or certainty.

It was the painful realization
that staying was costing me more
than leaving ever could.

I reached a point where I could no longer ignore
what my heart, my body, and my spirit
had been whispering for years:

This isn't life.
It's survival.
And my soul was ready for more.

That knowing didn't make me fearless.

But it made me willing.

And willingness was enough
to take the first step.

Sis... I didn't have all the answers.
But God went before me.

"I will go before you
and make the crooked places straight."
— Isaiah 45:2

And that's when I realized something important:
the choices shaping my life had to change.

<u>Choice One:</u>
I stopped choosing what felt familiar —
even when familiar felt easier.

Choice Two:
I began choosing more carefully —
paying attention to patterns I had ignored before.

Choosing differently didn't happen overnight.

Some days, I moved forward.
Some days, I slid back.

But here was the breakthrough:

I finally saw myself.
I recognized the pattern.
I stopped pretending.

Instead of demanding perfection,
I began making one honest choice at a time —
choices aligned with peace,
with truth,
and with the woman God was calling me to become.

And step by step...

I moved.

The Power of Choice

Accessing the Authority That Was Always Within Me

Sis... hear me for a moment.

Choice may look simple from the outside.
But on the inside, it is sacred work.

Choice is the quiet intersection
where pain meets possibility —
and direction is decided.

Not the familiar direction.
Not the comfortable one.

But the direction of:

- Peace

- Healing
- Alignment
- Identity
- Wholeness

There came a season when a simple truth became my anchor — something God used to steady my breath and guide my steps.

C.H.O.I.C.E.

Choose
Healing
Over
Internal
Chaos —
Every day.

Not once.
Not dramatically.

Every day.

Each morning, I began asking myself:

Am I choosing peace or turmoil?
Truth or denial?
Healing or comfort?
Faith or fear?
Boundaries or begging for respect?

Not perfectly.
Just honestly.

Because here is the deeper truth I had to face:

The power of choice was never missing.
I simply hadn't learned how to access it.

And Sis... that's true for so many of us.

Sometimes, pain has been making choices for us.

But Scripture reminds me:

**"I will instruct you and teach you in the way you should go;
I will counsel you with my loving eye on you."
— Psalm 32:8**

Choice didn't erase my pain.

But it opened a door
that suffering had convinced me was locked.

And every time I chose differently — even in small ways —
something shifted:

- a gentler thought
- a firmer boundary
- a quiet *not today*
- truth instead of pretending
- one small act of courage

And with each choice,
a link in the chain around my life loosened.

Sis, hear this — and **borrow these words if you need them:**

**"The power of choice is already within me.
I am simply learning to access
what has always been there."
— Rosita Perez**

This is what it looks like
to move from pain to power.

Just one honest choice at a time
in the direction of the woman
you are becoming.

A Moment Before We Continue

Sis... pause here with me.

We just walked through some of the deepest parts of my story —
not to relive them,
but to understand them.

I named ties I didn't create.
I told the truth about patterns I didn't see before.

That kind of honesty isn't small work.

It's sacred work.

And if parts of my story stirred something in you,
pay attention to that.

Because once we begin to see the patterns shaping our lives,
a deeper question naturally follows:

**Why do I keep walking back into the same emotional rooms —
even when I know what waits for me there?**

That's where we're headed next.

Because understanding *why* we return
is often the first step toward finally leaving.

In **Chapter 3**, I begin uncovering the deeper roots
behind those choices —
and how I learned to release them
with truth, grace, and growing strength.

For now...

Take one slow breath.

Let what surfaced settle.

**When you're ready,
pause for a moment with the Reflect & Renew page.**

And when it feels right...

we'll step into Chapter 3 — together.

Reflect & Renew

Releasing the Ties That Hold Me Back

1. Pause
Sis... take one slow breath.

Ask yourself:

What tie am I ready to release today?

Write one honest line.

One truth is enough
to begin letting go.

2. Truth to Hold
Some ties were never meant to be carried —
only released
so your heart can breathe again."
— Rosita Perez

For those who pray:
"Above all else, guard your heart,
for everything you do flows from it."
— Proverbs 4:23

3. One Small Step
Choose just one:

- Release one old vow
- Soften one reaction
- Small releases

create real freedom.

4. Your Encouraging Word
You are not bound to yesterday.

You are becoming the woman
who chooses freedom —

one breath,
one truth,
one step at a time.

C.H.O.I.C.E.

Choose
Healing
Over
Internal
Chaos —
Every day.

Not perfectly.
Just honestly.

CHAPTER 3

Why Do I Keep Living Here?

Uncovering the Real Reasons I Stayed in Painful Places

Sis... you've walked with me through some of the most courageous work of my life.

In **Chapter 1**, I named my house —
the emotional address I had been living in.

In **Chapter 2**, I uncovered the ties —
the unseen attachments that kept me there.

But now we step into the deepest question of all:

Why do I keep living here?

This is the chapter where so much finally begins to make sense.

Not because the answers are easy —
but because the patterns that once felt confusing
begin to reveal their *why*.

This chapter isn't about blame.
It isn't about shame.
And it's never about judging the woman I once was.

It's about understanding the woman inside who carried so much pain —
so I can finally set her free.

Because no woman stays in emotional pain for no reason.

There is always something beneath the surface:

A belief.
A memory.
A wound.
A loyalty.
A fear.
A story my younger self began living
long before she had words for it.

And Sis... here is something most women are rarely taught:

Sometimes we stay because our nervous system learned to call the familiar safe.

For a long time, I thought something was wrong with me.

But my brain wasn't betraying me —
it was protecting me with outdated information.

My heart wasn't broken —
it was carrying memories it never had the space to release.

My patterns weren't failures —
they were survival strategies that once helped me endure.

But survival is not the same as freedom.

In this chapter, I **uncover the deeper roots that shaped my choices** —
childhood moments, unspoken grief,
and quiet vows I didn't realize I had made.

Not to relive it.

But to redeem it.

You'll see my story, yes.

But more than that,
I hope you begin to recognize the hidden reasons
behind your own patterns.

Because when I could finally answer the question,

Why do I keep living here?

I became powerful enough
to choose something new.

Awareness is where freedom begins.

So before we go further, take this truth with you:

The roots may explain where we started.
But they don't get to decide where we grow.
— Rosita Perez

Deep breath, Sis.

We're going in —
and we're going in together.

Your breakthrough is waiting.

Types of Pain I Was Rooted In

The Wounds That Shaped My Patterns

This is the part of the journey many women avoid — including myself for decades.

Not because we are weak.

It's because looking beneath the surface
requires a different kind of courage.

And Sis... the fact that you're still here,
reading these pages,
tells me you carry that courage.

So come with me as we go deeper.

Now we ask the question that lives beneath the house itself:

What pain have I been rooted in —
without even realizing it?

Most of us grew roots long before we grew language.

We adapted before we understood.
We learned how to survive
before we ever felt safe.

And the patterns we carry today
are often connected to wounds
we never had the space to name.

Uncovering the Roots Beneath My Patterns

So let's begin uncovering some of the roots that quietly shaped my story.

As I began looking honestly at my life, I realized these roots were quietly shaping the patterns I kept repeating.

Childhood Loss & Emotional Displacement

One day, I was a fifteen-year-old daughter riding bikes.

The next, I was carrying responsibilities
that were never meant for a child.

I became the strong one.
The responsible one.
The one who kept going.

I learned to care for everyone else,
because I didn't know how to let anyone
care for the little girl in me.

Those beliefs didn't come from logic.
They were born from heartbreak.

These weren't bad habits.
They were survival roots.

**Survival may keep you alive —
but it cannot set you free.**

And when a child learns to survive too soon,
she often grows up afraid
of being left again.

Abandonment & Fear of Being Left

Losing my mother left an imprint
my younger heart didn't know how to name.

Years of heartbreak, betrayal, and emotional absence
quietly reinforced the same lie:

I'm not worth choosing.
I'm not worth staying for.

That belief followed me into adulthood.

It shaped my relationships,
my expectations,
and what I learned to tolerate.

I settled for love that didn't stay
because, without realizing it,
I didn't believe I was worth choosing.

The truth was, my relationship picker was broken.

Because unhealed wounds
have a way of taking over
and speaking loudly.

And when abandonment becomes a fear,
a woman often learns to protect herself
the only way she knows how.

The "Strong One" Identity

So I became strong.

Strong enough not to need.
Strong enough not to ask.
Strong enough not to break.

I never learned how to fall apart safely.

So I stopped:

expressing needs,
asking for help,
trusting anyone with my heart.

Strength became my armor.

And quietly,
it became my prison.

Because when strength becomes your identity,
softness can start to feel dangerous.

The Shame of "Not Enough"

Shame is the quietest root —
and often the deepest.

It doesn't shout.

It whispers:

You're the problem.
You're not lovable.
Be grateful for crumbs.

And when shame takes root,
a woman can begin shrinking her life
to fit what she believes she deserves.

For a long time,
I believed those whispers.

But slowly,
a new truth began to take root:

**"The lie of shame said I was not enough.
But the truth of healing reminds me
that I was never lacking — only wounded."
— Rosita Perez**

And once that truth began to surface,
something inside me shifted.

**What if I am worthy of more
than the life I've been settling for?**

Sis... if that question stirred something in you,
pause for a moment and listen to what your heart might be saying.

Write it down — and return to it later.

Because sometimes the first step toward moving forward
is simply recognizing the house you've been living in.

What I began to see were roots with deep claws —
patterns that had quietly shaped the life I was living.

They weren't random.

They were planted long before I had words
for what I was feeling.

And once I could finally see those roots clearly,
a deeper question began to surface.

How the Roots Revealed Themselves

Sis... for a long time, I avoided looking this far back.

I wanted healing,
but something in me hesitated —
afraid of what the truth might uncover.

But when I finally slowed down enough to listen,
God began showing me something
I had never fully understood.

As I traced my pain backward,
I didn't find just one root.

I found several.

Some formed in loss.
Some were shaped by survival.
And some grew into the patterns
I carried on just to keep going.

And slowly I began to understand something important:

**Tracing the origin of pain doesn't reopen the wound —
it reveals the doorway to healing.
— Rosita Perez**

This part of the journey isn't about blame
or revisiting the past to stay there.

It's about understanding — with compassion —
where my story first began to take shape.

Because when we begin to see those roots,
what once felt permanent can finally begin to loosen.

And as I looked honestly at my life,
two things began revealing themselves.

First, the **roots** —
the early experiences that shaped my emotional soil.

And then the **patterns** —
the ways I learned to survive what those roots created.

And slowly, awareness began to grow.

I started to see the connection
I had missed it for so many years.

The patterns that shaped my life
weren't random.

They had roots.

That awareness changed everything.

It allowed me to stop blaming who I became
and start understanding why.

What follows isn't meant to overwhelm you.

It's meant to help you see
how roots quietly grow patterns
long before we realize
they are shaping our lives.

The Roots of My Pain

Where the ground first cracked

Sis...

these are the roots that formed before I had words,
before I had choice,
before I knew how to protect myself.

They live in the body —
in the nervous system —
in the quiet places where a child learns
what feels safe,
what feels missing,
and what must be carried alone.

These roots are not about what I did wrong.

They are about what happened to me.

And once I could see that,
something inside me softened.

Because these roots explain
why so much of the rest of my life grew the way it did.

Root 1 — Early Loss

When my mother died,
the world I knew changed.

Life kept moving forward —
but something essential inside me paused.

I didn't just lose a mom.

I lost safety.
I lost the simple right
to be held
without having to be strong.

The little girl inside me quietly stepped aside
so the survivor in me could take over.

I learned to depend on myself early.

Anger helped me feel protected.
My quick wit became a way
to guard my heart.

For years,
I didn't realize how deeply
that loss shaped the woman I became.

Later, I learned something
that changed the way I saw myself.

Children who experience early loss
often grow into adults who over-function,
people-please,
or blame themselves —

not because something is wrong with them,

but because no child
was meant to carry
that kind of emotional weight.

Sis... that was me.

And if early loss touched your story too,
you may recognize pieces of yourself here —

not as a diagnosis,

but as an explanation.

And when love disappears early,
another root often grows beside it.

Root 2 — The Ache of Abandonment

The part of me that believed love leaves

I never said this out loud,
but abandonment shaped the way I loved.

It taught me to

hold on too tightly
tolerate too much
settle too often
overgive
hoping no one would walk away.

For a long time,
I didn't realize
I was still living from that wound.

Until one quiet moment —
a trembling moment —

when memories from years earlier surfaced.

Not to shame me.

But to show me
where the thread first began.

Right there,
I saw it clearly.

This wasn't about being needy,
or insecure,
or "too much."

It was about a younger version of me
trying to keep love
from leaving again.

And right there —
in that tender recognition —

God met me.

Not with corrections.
Not with answers.

But with presence.

For the first time in a long while,
I felt peace.

I felt hope.

It whispered,

You're not alone as you trace this pain.

And for the first time,
I felt safe enough
to keep going.

But some pain doesn't show itself
through fear of loss.

Sometimes it hides
in the grief we never allowed ourselves to feel.

Root 3 — Silent Grief

The tears I never allowed myself to cry

Grief that goes unspoken
doesn't disappear.

It settles.

It finds quiet places to live
when there is no room,
no permission,
no safety
to feel it fully.

I carried losses I never mourned:

my mother
my sense of safety
my childhood innocence
the version of love I hoped for
even parts of myself.

There were no rituals for this kind of grief.

No language.
No pause long enough
to let it move through me.

So I stayed composed.
Capable.
Strong.

But silent grief
has a way of showing up anyway.

It made me guarded.
Quick to anger.
Emotionally numb.
Bone-deep tired.

For years
I didn't call it grief.

I just thought
I needed to try harder,
be better,
hold it together longer.

But the truth is this:

It's hard to heal
what you never felt safe enough
to feel.

And naming that
was the beginning of compassion
for the woman I had been —

just trying
to survive.

The Patterns That Grew From Those Roots

Who I became to keep going

Sis...

this part of my story didn't begin with loss.

It began with adaptation.

After everything I had already been through,
I learned how to keep moving forward —
how to stay steady, capable, and strong.

Not because I was asked to.

Because life required it.

These ways of being weren't mistakes.

They were responses.

They helped me function,
carry responsibility,
and stay standing
when slowing down didn't feel like an option.

For a long time,
I didn't question who I had become.

I simply lived inside it.

Only later did I begin to notice
that some of these ways of being —
as helpful as they once were —
had grown heavy.

Not wrong.

Just heavy.

Becoming the One Who Handles Everything

The belief that everything depended on me

As a girl,
being needed made me feel valuable.

It was how I felt seen.
It was how I felt safe.

As a woman,
that same pattern followed me.

I became the fixer.
The strong one.
The rescuer.

The one who kept everything together
because control felt like protection.

Holding everything together
gave me a sense of order
in a world that once felt unpredictable.

That pattern ran deep.

It whispered:

If I handle everything, nothing will fall apart.
If I stay needed, I won't be left.

Sis... unknowingly that belief shaped years of my life.

Not because I wanted control.

But because being needed
was how I learned to feel secure.

And slowly I began to see
that surviving this way
had shaped who I believed myself to be.

The Identity I Outgrew

The version of me built on survival

I didn't notice it at first —
the way my identity had been shaped
by the very rooms I had lived in.

I became

the strong one
the dependable one
the overcomer
the caretaker
the survivor.

For a long time,
those names felt like honor.

They meant I could endure.

And for years,
that was enough.

Until it wasn't.

A quiet awareness began to grow.

Surviving
was no longer the same
as living.

I had learned how to endure.

But somewhere inside,
I began longing for something more.

Not just strength.

Freedom.

Freedom to discover
who I was beneath the roles,

beneath the responsibility,
beneath the armor I had built to survive.

The Beliefs That Helped Me Cope

The truths I lived by — even when they kept me stuck

These weren't beliefs
I consciously chose.

They formed quietly
in the same seasons
where I learned how to survive.

I learned:

I have to be strong.
That's how I'm respected.
That's how I'm loved.

Whoever I love will eventually leave.
So I stay guarded.
I stay prepared.

I have to take care of myself —
because no one else will.

These beliefs didn't come from imagination.

They came from experience.

For a long time,
they did exactly what they were meant to do.

They protected me.
They carried me.
They helped me keep going.

And now,
I can honor them
without letting them lead my life.

Because I AM a woman BEcoming.

And I no longer want to live only in survival.

What once helped me cope
doesn't have to guide every step anymore.

And that realization
feels like the beginning
of something gentler.

And true.

Where My Roots and Patterns Led Me

Sis...

for a long time
I thought I was simply choosing the wrong people.

That somehow
I kept missing the mark.

I called myself too forgiving,
too loyal,
too hopeful —

as if those were flaws
instead of clues.

What I couldn't see then
was that long before I chose a partner —

before I ever said *yes*,
or *I do*,
or *maybe this time* —

I was already carrying something into the room.

I didn't walk into relationships empty-handed.

I walked in carrying roots
I had never named.

Patterns
I believed were simply part of my personality.

Survival skills
I had learned early —
and later mistook for love.

At the time,
it felt like chemistry.

Desire.
Hope.

But underneath all of that,
something quieter was shaping my steps.

Not because I was broken.
Not because I lacked discernment.

But because what grows underground
always influences
what reaches for the light.

And once I slowed down enough to see that,
I began to understand how those same roots
showed up again and again —

in dating,
in deep love,
and eventually in marriage.

That awareness didn't condemn me.

It grounded me.

Because when you can name
what you've been carrying,
you can finally decide
what you're ready
to set down.

Let me gently show you
how those roots appeared in my relationships.

When Abandonment Shaped My Love

When someone didn't call back,
I felt it in my body.

My chest tightened.
My thoughts raced.

When someone pulled away,
I reached for them.

When someone treated me poorly,
I told myself a story
that made it make sense.

Not because I didn't know better.

But because a part of me still believed
love was something you could lose
if you didn't hold it tightly enough.

Because I lost my mother early

I didn't connect that loss
to the way I showed up in relationships.

But it was there.

In how quickly I attached.
In how much I tolerated.
In how afraid I was
to be the one left standing.

Looking back now,
I can see it more clearly.

I wasn't weak.

I was trying to protect myself
from a loss
I had already lived through once.

When Responsibility Became My Role

This pattern showed up quietly.

I noticed it
in how much I did.

I filled the gaps.
I smoothed things over.
I explained what didn't feel right.

I stayed longer than I should have.

I apologized
even when I didn't know why.

Somewhere along the way
I became the fixer.

The one who understood.
The one who kept the peace.
The one who carried what no one else wanted to hold.

And here's the truth
I didn't know how to say back then:

I believed that if I could just be necessary enough,
love would stay.

Not because I wanted control.

**But because I had learned early
that love felt safest
when I was useful.**

Looking back now
I can see it clearly.

I wasn't building connection.

I was managing it.

And love that has to be managed
isn't love at all.

When Grief Went Underground

My grief didn't disappear.

It went underground.

And the cost of not grieving
showed up in my relationships.

I pushed the pain down
and kept moving.

I learned how to function.
How to stay strong.
How to build walls
that kept the pain at a distance.

What I didn't understand then
was that those same walls
also kept love out.

For a long time,
I couldn't see the connection.

I just knew that sometimes,
I held on too tightly.

And other times,
I pulled away without warning.

Both were symptoms —

not of who I was,

but of what I had survived.

Sis... I wish someone had told me earlier:

**Your roots shaped you,
but they do not get to strangle
who you're becoming.**

And when I finally began untangling them,
I realized something life-changing:

I wasn't attracting the wrong men.

I was attracting
what felt familiar
to the unhealed parts of me.

But now?

Now I was learning
to choose differently.

And that awareness
gave me room to choose.

What I Was Carrying — And What I Was Ready to Set Down

Sis...

understanding my roots didn't change my past —
but it changed how I held it.

For the first time, I could see my story
without defending it,
without minimizing it,
and without blaming myself for what I survived.

Those roots weren't character flaws.

They were responses.

Formed in loss.
Strengthened in survival.
Carried quietly into relationships
where they once tried to protect me —
even when they no longer served me.

I didn't carry them because I was broken.

I carried them because they were familiar.

Because they helped me endure
what I didn't yet know how to grieve,
name,
or release.

And seeing that softened something in me.

I stopped asking,

What's wrong with me?

And began asking a braver question:

What did I learn —
and what am I ready to unlearn?

Because awareness doesn't demand change.

It invites it.

And that invitation led me somewhere new —

not to a decision yet,

but to a willingness.

A willingness to accept what shaped me
without letting it define me.

A willingness to believe
that healing could be chosen —
not earned through more pain.

This is where growth begins.

Not with force.
Not with pressure.

But with the quiet courage
to see clearly
and choose honestly.

When Acceptance Began

Sis...

once the truth was named,
I couldn't unknow it.

I could feel the pull
to do what I had always done —

adjust,
endure,
explain,
survive.

But something had shifted.

Not around me.

Inside me.

For the first time,
I wasn't asking,

How do I make this work?

I was asking something deeper:

What happens if I stop fighting
what I already know?

Acceptance didn't arrive as relief.

It arrived as honesty.

The kind of honesty
that stops negotiating with pain
and starts listening to

what it has been trying to show me.

And that is where healing begins.
Not with dramatic decisions —
but with the quiet courage

to stop living on autopilot
and choose differently.

Once I could see the truth
of what I had been carrying,
I could no longer unsee it.

And from that moment on,
change was no longer avoidable.

Reflect & Renew

Letting Go of What I Carried

1. Pause & Reflect
Sis...you've just walked through some deep places.

Take one slow breath.
Place your hand over your heart.

Ask yourself gently:

What root am I still holding
that no longer belongs to me?

Don't analyze it.
Don't force an answer.

Just notice what rises.

Write **one honest sentence.**

Because honesty is where healing begins.

2. Truth to Hold
"Understanding the origin of my pain didn't reopen the wound — it revealed the doorway to my healing."
— Rosita Perez

Let this truth settle in:

You are not revisiting pain.
You are opening the door to healing.

3. One Small Step
Choose just one:

- Tell yourself the truth about one relationship or pattern
- Give yourself permission to grieve something you never allowed yourself to grieve

Small steps shift the direction of a life.

4. An Encouraging Word
Sis...
I honor the work you just did.

Tracing your roots isn't weakness —
it's wisdom.

You faced truths that many women avoid for decades.
You looked at old wounds with new compassion.

Hear this clearly:

**Your roots may explain your patterns,
but they do not define your future.**

You are not bound to what shaped you.

You are free to become the woman
you were always meant to be.

And the courage rising in you now?

That is the beginning of your next step.

CHAPTER 4

Am I Ready to Move?

The Courage to Step Into Something New

Realizing the truth about my roots and patterns didn't instantly change my life.

What it did instead was place a new tension in my heart.

Because once you understand what has been shaping your life —
the patterns you've lived inside,
the ties you've carried,
the ways you've learned to survive —

a deeper question begins to surface.

Not loudly.
Not all at once.
But steadily.

If I can see what's no longer working...
am I ready to live differently?

That question is where real change begins.

And this chapter lives in that moment —
the space between awareness and courage.

Because before a woman moves into a new life,
she first has to recognize
what staying has been quietly costing her.

The Hidden Costs of Staying Too Long

We don't talk enough about the quiet losses
a woman carries
when she stays in a place she has already outgrown.

Those losses rarely arrive all at once.

They come slowly —
subtly, almost politely.

My peace began to leak.
My confidence thinned.
My voice grew quiet —
not because I lacked truth,
but because silence felt safer.

My identity bent
to fit walls that were never built
for my becoming.

And the hardest part?

I began mourning myself
while I was still breathing.

Because eventually
the emotional bill comes due.

Every time you remain in a place
that no longer has room
for who you are becoming,

you pay —

not all at once,

but in pieces
of yourself.

When Does Staying Cost Too Much?

Eventually, a woman begins to notice
what staying is costing her.

For me, there came a moment
when staying was no longer stable.

It was more self-abandonment.

Not because I didn't try hard enough.
Not because I didn't pray, endure, compromise, or hope.

But because something inside me knew:

This place is costing me more than it's giving.

That knowing didn't arrive loudly.

It came quietly —
like a slow leak in my soul.

I gave pieces of myself away
to keep the peace.

I lost my voice
one silent compromise at a time.

And slowly, a truth surfaced
I had never said out loud:

I didn't fall out of love.

I faded out of myself.

Until one night, standing alone
in the room I was now sleeping in,
another truth followed close behind:

Staying wasn't saving us.

Staying was erasing me.

And once I could name that cost,
I could no longer ignore it.

Because staying should never require
abandoning the woman I was becoming.

I can't keep living in rooms
that were never built
for who I'm becoming.
— Rosita Perez

Acceptance Isn't Giving Up — It's Waking Up

For years, I thought I could fix everything
with prayer, patience, and endurance.

Because I believed in marriage.
I honored my vows.

I believed commitment could resurrect
what was slowly dying.

I believed God would restore
what was broken.

And Sis... hear this clearly:

I still believe in marriage.
I still honor what it stands for.

Leaving was the last thing I ever wanted.

But somewhere along the way,
I began sacrificing myself
to keep it alive.

I stopped speaking up.
I shrank my needs.
I softened my truths.

I endured
because endurance had always been
my default setting.

Until one day
I looked in the mirror
and didn't recognize the woman staring back at me.

She was tired.
Small.
Disappearing.

That's when I understood something
I had resisted for a long time.

Acceptance isn't giving up.

It's waking up.

**I learned that I couldn't heal
in the same place
that kept breaking me.
— Rosita Perez**

How Fear Quietly Controlled Me

When my marriage entered its hardest season,
fear was the loudest voice in the room.

My mind filled with thoughts like:

You stayed for the kids —
they saw how toxic it became,
and the blame landed on you.

This is the best you'll get.
Don't leave — just survive.
You may be alone forever.

And Sis... fear didn't start there.

Looking back, I can see how long it had been shaping my life —
long before my marriage reached that breaking point.

Fear taught me to wear masks.
To hide emotion.
To appear strong
even when I was breaking inside.

I became skilled at managing fear
because fear was part of who I was.

I knew its patterns.
Its rules.
How to survive within it.

Leaving felt riskier
than staying in pain.

Until one day...
the pain of staying
finally outweighed
the fear of moving.

For the first time, I allowed myself to ask a different question:

If fear wasn't calling the shots...
how would my life be different?

That question didn't give me instant answers.

But it opened a doorway.

What Would Life Look Like Without Fear in Control?

Imagining the Freedom Fear Tried to Hide

Sis... can I tell you the truth about fear?

For most of my life, fear didn't show up as danger —
it showed up as protection.

It whispered things like:

Stay small.
Stay quiet.
Don't rock the boat.
Don't hope too much... don't want too much.

Fear convinced me that if I stayed careful,
if I stayed in control,
I wouldn't get hurt.

But slowly, quietly,
fear became the very thing hurting me.

Fear shaped my choices.
Fear narrowed my world.
Fear helped build the emotional houses I lived in.

It told me to tolerate relationships that were breaking me.

That chaos was better than being alone.

That my worth depended on someone choosing me.

That I wasn't enough —
strong enough,
smart enough,
lovable enough.

Fear had been driving for so long
I didn't even realize freedom existed.

Everything began to shift the moment I asked a different question:

What if fear isn't the one steering anymore?

What if peace took the wheel?
What if courage led the way?

What if trust set the pace?

What if I didn't need certainty to move forward —
only willingness?

That question didn't give me instant answers.

But it opened a doorway
to a different life.

What If Pain Is Pushing You Forward?

Sis... here's a truth many of us were never taught:

Pain isn't always the enemy.

Sometimes it's the messenger —
the nudge that opens the doorway.

For most of my life,
I treated pain as something to endure, silence, or pray away.

I never stopped long enough to ask it a question:

What if this pain isn't here to punish me —
but to push me toward the woman I'm becoming?

Because the breaking point —
the moment you whisper,

I can't live like this anymore —

often arrives just before the breakthrough.

I was breaking.

Not because I was weak.

But because my soul was tired
of carrying what was never mine.

For the first time,
I didn't run from the ache
or hide it behind strength.

I listened.

And what I heard was simple:

My pain wasn't betraying me.

It was guiding me.

Sometimes pain isn't breaking you.

It's breaking you free.

Pain Is Not Punishment — It's Information

Sis... hear this gently:

Pain is often the soul's first language.

It speaks when my mind refuses the truth.
It whispers when I ignore the signs.
It tightens my chest when I'm settling.
It steals my sleep when my spirit needs change.

Pain says:

- You've outgrown this.
- This isn't love.
- You're disappearing.
- This isn't who you are.

For years, I asked the wrong question:

Why me?

But the turning point came
when I asked a different one:

What is this pain trying to tell me?

The answers were quiet —
but undeniable.

I'm carrying too much.
I'm pretending to be okay.
I'm abandoning myself to stay.

And once I understood
what the pain was revealing,

I didn't feel defeated.

I felt awake.

Because pain may knock you down —

but fear doesn't get to keep you there.

What If My Turning Point Is Closer Than I Think?

Sis... I know how exhausting it is to be strong.

I know what it feels like to carry pain so long
it starts to feel familiar.

But here is the truth I didn't realize for a long time:

I am allowed to walk away from what wounds me.

I am allowed to release what drains me.
I am allowed to rise when staying is killing my spirit.

My breaking point wasn't the end.

It was the beginning.

The moment my soul tapped me on the shoulder and whispered,
It's time.

Time to

- breathe again.
- heal again.
- choose myself again.
- step into the life that had been waiting for me.

Pain pushed me forward.

And maybe — just maybe —
it wasn't breaking me at all.

Sometimes pain isn't breaking you —
it's breaking you free.
— Rosita Perez

Dreaming Beyond the Damage Isn't Denial — It's Courage

For a long time, I believed dreaming again
meant pretending the pain never happened.

But now I know better.

Dreaming isn't denial.

It's courage.

It's the courage to stand in the middle of
what tried to break you and say:

Something beautiful can still rise from this.

There was a scripture that breathed possibility
back into my soul:

"God will restore the years the locusts have eaten."
— Joel 2:25

That promise doesn't mean God rewinds time
or gives us back the past exactly as it was.

It means something deeper.

God doesn't erase the damage.

He redeems it.

He takes what was stripped away
and grows something new in its place.

Not a copy of what was lost —

but a future strengthened
by everything we survived.

Hope is the first seed you plant
in the soil where pain once lived.

The Awakening That Changed Everything

There was a day — early in my healing —
when I was walking to my mailbox.

The sun met my face in a way that felt personal,
like God brushing my cheek with kindness.

Out of nowhere, a vision rose inside me:

Me — smiling.
Free.
Unafraid.
At peace.

A version of myself
I hadn't seen in years.

That image didn't come
because I suddenly felt strong.

It came because I was finally present.
Finally, quiet enough to listen.

And what I received was this:
"Rosita... peace and joy are already yours."

Not something I had to earn.
Not something I had to prove myself worthy of.

Something waiting for me
the moment I stopped surviving,
and allowed myself to receive.

The Courage to Step Into Something New

Sis... by the time a woman reaches this moment,
something inside her is already stirring.

Maybe it's a whisper.
Maybe it's a quiet knowing.

Maybe it's a deep ache that says:

This can't be my whole life.

And sooner or later,
that stirring becomes a question:

Am I ready to move?

Not just physically.

Emotionally.
Spiritually.
Mentally.
Identity-deep.

Because moving isn't just about leaving a place.

It's about stepping toward a future
you've only imagined.

And courage doesn't always look like confidence.

Sometimes it looks like shaking hands,
wobbly knees,
and a quiet whisper:

I can't stay here anymore.

**"Courage doesn't always roar.
Sometimes it sounds like a woman finally telling herself the truth."
— Rosita Perez**

Who's Walking With You on the Way?

Sis... here's a truth I had to learn the hard way:

**Isolation cannot carry you
where healing is trying to take you.**

Many of us have been wounded — deeply.
By family.
By friends.
By partners.
By people we trusted.

When betrayal hits the soul,
our first instinct is protection.

I shrank.
I shut down.

Not because I didn't crave connection —
but because connection had once cost me too much.

But healing began the moment
I found the courage
to step back into community.

Because the truth is simple:

We were never meant to heal alone.

"Two are better than one...
because they have a good return for their labor."
— Ecclesiastes 4:9

The right people don't drain your strength.

They steady you
while you find it again.

Why I Know Freedom Is Possible

Let me share this not to elevate myself,
but to offer living proof
that freedom is possible.

For years, I was stubborn.

But my stubbornness wasn't strength.
It was fear of the unknown
and a need to stay in control.

And still...
God never stopped meeting me.

Sometimes, He strengthened me.
Sometimes, He carried me.
Sometimes, He simply sat with me
in the quiet
when I had no words left.

And then one day...
the whisper came:

Enough.

Not harsh.
Not angry.
Not demanding.

Loving.
Clear.
Certain.

It marked the moment
I stopped resisting
and began releasing.

Not everything changed overnight —
but something shifted forever.

That whisper wasn't about failure.

It was permission.

Permission to stop surviving.
Permission to stop negotiating with fear.
Permission to choose freedom
one honest step at a time.

And that's why I believe this truth
for every woman reading these pages:

Freedom isn't reserved
for the brave or the perfect.

It begins the moment a woman
is willing to become
who God created her to be.

And the same God
who met me there

is ready to meet
every woman
who is willing
to take the first step.

Now I Turn the Question Toward You

Sis... pause here for a moment.

After everything you've just read,
what might be stirring inside you?

What possibilities feel closer than they once did?
What boundaries might finally feel necessary — even kind?
What dreams have been waiting quietly for your attention?

You don't have to answer all of that today.

Just allowing yourself
to ask these questions honestly
is enough for now.

Because freedom rarely begins
with certainty.

It begins the moment
a woman is willing
to wonder
if more is possible.

Saying Yes to the Woman Within

For years, I survived.

I endured.
I adjusted.
I pushed.
I smiled.
I kept everything together.

But beneath all of that,

another version of me
was waiting.

Not the wounded one.
Not the silenced one.

The woman I was always meant to be.

Steady.
Whole.
Grounded.
Clear.
Loved.

And free.

Saying yes to her didn't mean
I had everything figured out.

It didn't mean fear disappeared.

It meant I stopped resisting
the woman God designed me to be.

And that one yes —
even whispered —

set everything in motion.

Stepping Into Readiness

Sis... take one slow breath.

Notice what you've just walked through.

You faced fear.
You told the truth about what staying has cost you.
You listened to your pain.

And maybe — even quietly —
you said yes to the woman rising within you.

That is readiness.

Readiness isn't loud.

It's the quiet knowing that says:

I can't stay where I've been...
and I'm willing to move.

You're standing at the doorway.

And sometimes all it takes
to step through that doorway
is one small yes.

"Becoming the woman you're called to be begins with one small yes — and that yes changes everything."
— Rosita Perez

Reflect & Renew

Readiness Begins Here

1. Pause & Reflect
Sis... place a hand over your heart.
Take one slow breath in... and out.

Ask yourself gently:

What might my life look like
if fear no longer led my choices?

Write one honest sentence.

That's enough.

2. Truth to Hold
"Be strong and courageous... for the Lord your God is with you wherever you go."
—Joshua 1:9

"Readiness isn't loud — it's the quiet moment your spirit whispers, *I can't stay where I am.*"
— Rosita Perez

3. One Small Step
Choose just one:

- Say out loud: **"Fear doesn't choose for me."**
- Share one honest truth with someone safe.

Small steps shift entire futures.

4. An Encouraging Word
You faced the truth.
You felt the fear.

And you didn't turn away.

You are becoming the woman
your pain once tried to silence —

steady,
brave,
rising in your own time.

Take your next step with courage.

You are closer than you think.

Sis... pause for a moment
and notice how far you've come.

Pat yourself on your back!

You've faced truth.
You've loosened the ties that once held you still.
And you've said yes — even quietly —
to the woman you are becoming.

But healing doesn't end with release.

It leads somewhere.

So when you're ready,
turn the page.

You've begun healing inwardly.

Now you get to live outwardly.

CHAPTER 5

That's It — I'm Moving

Stepping Boldly Into My Next Chapter

Sis... let me bring you into the exact moment everything shifted for me.

I had done the work.
I had faced the truth.
I had loosened the ties.
I had confronted fear.

I had said yes to understanding and loving the woman inside me who had been waiting for decades.

And still — I stood at a fork in the road... terrified.

Because even when your spirit is ready, your body and brain don't let go so easily.

Your healing says, "Move forward."
Your fear says, "Stay where it's familiar."

I remember sitting there thinking:

"I know I'll be healthier...
I know life will be better...
so why does stepping forward feel so hard?"

Have you felt that?

That strange tug where your mind knows the truth,
but your body clings to the only patterns it has ever known?

It's real.
It's normal.
And it's part of the journey.

My brain was loud:
"Stay here. It's safer. You know this pain. You can handle this chaos."

But something deeper in me — the part God kept strengthening, the part healing kept awakening — whispered back:

"Go.
This season is over.
Not everyone can come with you.
And that's okay."

That whisper didn't shout.
It nudged.
It breathed.
It reminded me that the people who fell away weren't punishments — they were protection.

Because the next season, God was calling me into required new strength, new patterns, and new voices.

And then a new truth formed in my spirit:

"This step isn't just about me.
It's about my daughter.
My grandchildren.
My lineage.
My legacy."

Sis... this is what I need you to hear:

Every time a woman chooses healing,
she breaks a generational pattern.

Every time a woman chooses courage,
she shifts the atmosphere her family lives in.

Every time she chooses truth,
she creates freedom her daughters and sons may never have to fight for.

This moment — this fork in the road — is bigger than you.

It's your legacy whispering,
Choose differently.

And if I'm honest...
there were many moments when I wanted to sabotage my own healing.

Old patterns are familiar.
They call me when the path forward feels uncertain.

But something stronger inside me kept whispering back:

No. You've come too far to turn around now.

So, Sis...
come with me.

Let me walk you through challenges and the steps that helped me choose a new path — one that leads toward freedom.

The Fork in My Road

If I turned left, I would return to what I knew.
The same reactions.
The same fears.
The same emotional houses.

The same generational patterns replayed in the next generation.

It wasn't healthy.
It wasn't peaceful.
It wasn't aligned.

But it was familiar.

If I turned right, I would walk — trembling but determined — into possibility.

Into healing.
Into peace.

Into identity.
Into purpose.

Into a life I had never seen modeled... but deeply longed for.

And Sis... my pain had run its course.
It had nothing left to teach me.

The pain finally outweighed the fear.

So I chose to turn right.
I chose forward.

I chose me.

And that's what Chapter 5 invites you to do:

To choose the direction that leads to your becoming.

This is your fork in the road.

This book didn't hand you perfection.
It handed you permission.

It didn't give you answers.
It gave you access.

It didn't promise ease.
It promised transformation.

And now?

You have the power of choice.

To move forward.
To break old patterns.
To rewrite your story.
To heal what was handed to you.

To leave a legacy that blesses the generations after you.

Hear me clearly, Sis...

You can do this.
You're ready.
You've already begun.

So please —
don't give up on yourself now.

My Yes Came Quietly — Through Tears

For me, saying yes wasn't loud.

It didn't happen in a prayer meeting, a sermon,
or some dramatic breakthrough.

It came on an ordinary day —
when I was finally exhausted by my own patterns.

Under my breath, I whispered,

"I'm tired of this."

And something deep in my spirit whispered back,
Finally.

That quiet yes didn't fix everything.

But it set everything in motion.

Because my yes didn't have to be strong.

It just had to be honest.

Crossing the Threshold

The moment you decide, "I'm not going back."

Sis... nobody tells you this:

You rarely feel ready when it's time to move.

Most breakthroughs don't arrive as confidence.
They arrive as a quiet knowing —
the moment you finally admit,

I can't stay here anymore.

Fear was still present when I reached that threshold.
It just no longer had the final word.

Because readiness isn't a feeling.

It's a decision.

When I reached the end of what I could carry alone,
I asked God to meet me
right where I was still afraid.

There were no fireworks.
No dramatic signs.

Fear didn't disappear.

But I learned something important:

You don't move because fear is gone.
You move because staying no longer fits
the woman you're becoming.

And the moment you take even one honest step forward,
fear begins to lose the power it once held over you.

Saying Yes Doesn't Require Perfection — Only Permission

Sis... hear this with your heart:

Saying yes didn't mean
I had everything figured out.

It didn't mean the fear was gone.
It didn't mean I suddenly felt brave.

It meant I stopped resisting
the woman God designed me to be.

It meant choosing healing over habit.
Growth over survival.

Courage over comfort.
Truth over pretending.

**It meant giving myself permission
to rise.**

And that one yes —
even whispered —

began a shift
heaven couldn't ignore.

Learning to Trust Peace

After my divorce, I thought healing would feel light —
like waking up free and whole.

Instead, I woke up to a silence that felt unfamiliar.

I had chosen freedom.
But my body was still catching up.

**After long seasons of emotional stress,
the nervous system doesn't immediately recognize peace.**

It has been trained to expect chaos.

So when the quiet finally arrives,
it can feel strange —
even unsettling.

But that discomfort isn't failure.

It's an adjustment.

My unease wasn't a sign I was going backward.
It was my body learning a new way to live.

So I stopped questioning my decision,
and started honoring the process.

I wasn't meant to rush peace.

I was meant to practice it.

And little by little,
quiet stopped feeling empty.

It began to feel safe.

And for the first time in a long while, I realized I wasn't just leaving an old life behind — I was learning how to live in a new one.

How I Found Community Again

Sis... I wasn't searching for community.
I was simply showing up to support a friend.

But something shifted the moment I sat in that room.

Women were sharing openly —
hurt, tears, stories still tender.

Not perfect, but present.
Not polished, but real.

And for the first time in a long while,
I felt how heavy life had become
to carry alone.

Still, I didn't rush in.

I listened more than I spoke.
Shared pieces, not everything.
Kept my heart close, because trust still felt fragile.

But little by little, something became clear.

They saw me.
They didn't rush me.
They didn't judge me.

And slowly, it felt like God was inviting me
out of hiding.

Then came one of those unmistakable confirmations.

For two days in a row, I opened a podcast or YouTube video at random —
and each time the message was the same:

Not everyone can go where you're going.
Some people had to be released for your protection.

By the third time, I paused.
I've learned that when a message repeats,
it's not coincidence—
it's confirmation of what your spirit already knows.

For me, it felt like God aligning my heart
with the people HE knew I needed.

Because the truth is simple, Sis:

We were never designed to heal alone.

Looking back now, I can see the path more clearly.

I shared the moment of decision.
The threshold where I chose not to go back.
The adjustments that came as my heart and mind learned a new way to live.

And the support God placed around me when I needed it most.

But that was only the beginning.

Because understanding the journey is one thing.

Learning how to live differently is another.

And in the next part of my story,
life didn't just feel different —

it began to change.

Rebuilding a New Way of Living

New Habits for a New Woman

Sis… choosing to move forward was only the beginning.

The real transformation happened in the quiet days that followed — when I had to learn how to live differently.

Because healing doesn't just change what you understand.
It changes what you practice.

For years, my habits had been shaped by survival —
patterns learned in pain, repeated out of familiarity.

But a new life requires new ways of living.

Not perfection.
Not overnight change.

Just small, honest choices
that begin to align your life
with the woman you're becoming.

Small actions that anchor identity and reinforce change

Sis… here's what I learned the hard way:

Becoming a new woman isn't a moment.
It's a muscle.

Healing gave me awareness.
But habits gave me transformation.

Awareness whispered,
You deserve peace.

But my patterns were trained for chaos—
and without new practices,
I kept walking back into what my heart had already outgrown.

I wanted a breakthrough,
but I was still using survival behaviors
to build a healed life.

It doesn't work.

You can't create a healed life
with old reflexes.

And if you're honest, Sis...
you've felt this too.

Where This Became Real for Me

As my healing journey unfolded, I started looking more honestly at the unhealthy patterns in my life. What I eventually discovered — and had to accept — was that I struggled with love addiction.

Now it was beginning to make sense. The way I gave and received love had brought me a lot of pain, and I knew I needed to understand why, so I could break that pattern.

Before I healed from this pattern, love addiction looked like this in my life:

The ache to belong.
The longing to be chosen.
The need to be needed.

Even at my own expense.

Affection felt like oxygen.
Attention felt like security.
And chaos often felt like connection.

Even as a Christian —
even while praying and serving —
parts of me were still reaching for validation
in places God had never sent me.

Healing didn't make me perfect.
It simply revealed where my heart had still been aching.

And maybe that was the most human part of all.

That season no longer defines me. I am healed and no longer bound by those patterns or love addiction, and God now uses my story to help other women find freedom.

And that freedom required me to learn a new way of living.

The Emotional Houses & Rooms

Part of being human was not realizing how long I had been living inside destructive emotional houses.

Houses like:

- **The House of Silence and Strength** — where I learned to hide my pain and carry on.
- **The House of Crumbs** — where I accepted less than I deserved.
- **The House of Survival** — where pain became normal.
- **The House of Compromise** — where I traded pieces of myself to avoid abandonment.
- **The House of Conflict & Codependence** — where chaos felt like intimacy.

But the hardest truth was this:

I kept returning to rooms
I had already prayed to leave.

Not because they were healthy —
but because they were familiar.

Inside those houses were rooms I knew too well:

- The room of self-betrayal — where I silenced my needs.
- The room of over-functioning — where I carried more than was mine.
- The room of settling — where I tolerated neglect.

- The room of **confusing love with sacrifice** — where sacrifice and love looked the same.

Sis...

I didn't stay because I didn't want better.

I stayed because I didn't yet know
how to live differently.

But here's the part that confronted me most:

I kept moving back into rooms
I had prayed to leave —
because they felt familiar,
even while they were quietly destroying me.

A Generational Truth I Had to Face

Some of those rooms weren't built by me —
they were handed to me.

Patterns I watched growing up.
Messages modeled but never spoken.
Sacrifice framed as survival.
Silence dressed as loyalty.
Over-functioning mistaken for strength.

**Some of those rooms were inherited —
family heirlooms disguised as coping.**

But this truth changed everything:

Just because something was normal in my past
doesn't mean it is my inheritance.

A new life required me
to break old leases
and refuse generational floor plans
that never fit the woman God designed me to be.

And then God whispered something that stayed with me:

Leaving the old you behind
means dismantling the structures
that taught you to stay small.

That meant not renovating those rooms —
but demolishing them.

Not repainting the house —
but moving out of it.

Not praying for change
while living in the same patterns —
but tearing up the floorboards
that had held me hostage.

Sis... this is why habits matter.

They don't just change behavior.

They dismantle the architecture
of who pain taught you to be.

New Habits for a New Woman

These weren't polished spiritual disciplines.

They were gritty recovery practices.

Walking away from what hurt me
felt like withdrawal.

Choosing myself
felt like rebellion.

Sitting alone
felt like failure.

And I wish someone had told me this sooner:

Becoming healthy often feels worse
before it feels better.

Growth isn't glamorous.

It's the daily tension
between who you were
and who you're becoming.

Even with faith.
Even with revelation.
Even when you know better.

There were days I whispered,

"God... I don't want to go back.
But moving forward is hard too.
Give me the strength to keep going."

Sis... hear this:

When it feels hard, don't quit.

You're not breaking.

You're becoming.

What I Learned

New habits don't just stabilize you.
They rebuild you.

Because escaping captivity
is not the same as refusing to return.

So I created non-negotiables —
internal guardrails that protected my healing:

- Telling myself the truth
- Stepping away from chaos
- Resting without guilt
- Asking for help without shame
- Trusting my intuition

Not to be perfect.

But to stay present.

These habits didn't erase the urge to go back —
they strengthened my ability to keep moving forward.

And yes... it was hard.

Because some of us aren't just changing behaviors.

We're dismantling the structure built from
inherited patterns,
survival beliefs,
and the lie that shrinking is the price of love.

Sis... hear me:

Tearing down that old structure
is not optional.

**Your past doesn't get the final word
on the woman you are becoming.**

What wounded you does not define you.

It prepared you.

You are worth the work.

And Sis...
you are not just breaking patterns —

you are rebuilding who you were always meant to be.

The Woman Inside Me Has Been Waiting

I didn't ignore her on purpose.

I was busy surviving.
Busy meeting everyone else's needs.
Busy carrying homes, marriages, work, responsibilities,
and expectations on my back.

I kept telling myself,
I'll get to me later.

But later never came.

Pain was familiar.
Fear was predictable.
And shrinking felt safer than rising.

I knew that life.
I had lived it for decades.

Enduring quietly.
Keeping the peace.
Staying small enough
to hold everything together.

Until one day, I asked myself a question
I could no longer avoid:

Is this the life I want to keep living?

My honest answer
changed everything.

Living Boldly in My Becoming

Standing in identity without apology.

This is where everything began to come together.

Not as habits to master.
Not as rules to remember.

But as a new way of standing.

I didn't become bold because I perfected my healing.

I became bold because I chose to stand where I was — on purpose.

I protected my peace.
I strengthened my joy.
I released what no longer belonged.

And from that place, something shifted.

I stopped asking for permission
to take up space in my own life.

I stopped shrinking my voice
to make others comfortable.

I stopped second-guessing decisions
that aligned with who I was becoming.

Living boldly didn't mean becoming louder.

It meant becoming truer.

I began speaking from conviction instead of fear.
Choosing out of clarity instead of guilt.

This is what identity feels like
when it is no longer buried under survival.

Steady.
Grounded.
Rooted.

Where fear once led, purpose now guides.
Where hesitation once lived, trust has taken its place.

God did not give me a spirit of fear.
HE gave me power, love, and a sound mind.

And when I began to see myself through His eyes,
I realized something profound:

I was never broken.

I was becoming.

A new thing was unfolding—
not rushed, not forced,
but intentional and true.

Living boldly isn't about having all the answers.

It's about walking forward aligned with who you are now —
shoulders back,

heart open,
feet planted.

This is what it looks like to live from identity instead of pain.
From truth instead of habit.
From becoming instead of fear.

These were not the only choices that shaped my healing —
but they were the ones that mattered most in this season.

Reflect & Renew

Walking Boldly Into What's Next

1. Pause & Reflect
Sis... pause.

Place one hand over your heart.
Take one slow breath in, and release it.

Ask yourself gently:

**Where am I standing now —
and how does it feel to stand here?**

Write one honest sentence.

That's enough.

2. Truth to Hold
You are not starting over.

You are standing on ground
you fought to reach.

Becoming doesn't require perfection.

It requires presence.

And you are here.

3. One Small Step
Choose one step
that honors the woman you are becoming.

It might be:

- Saying no without explaining
- Resting without guilt
- Choosing peace over familiarity

Write it down.

Small steps are how brave women move forward.

4. An Encouraging Word
Sis... you didn't quit.

You didn't go back.

You chose truth.
You chose courage.

And now you stand here —
stronger and more aligned than before.

Walk forward.

Sis, You are ready for what's next.

A Final Word From My Heart to Yours

My journey from pain to power took me through every emotion imaginable and challenged me to the very depths of who I thought I was.

For a long time, I fit—because I was living for who the world said I should be.

Until one day...
I no longer fit.

I made the choice to heal, and it has been one of the most challenging things I have ever done.

There were days I honestly did not think I would make it. Days when the pain felt so overwhelming that I asked God to take me because I was unsure I could survive the journey to the other side.

But God would not let me give up.

So I did my work.

Today, my battle scars tell a story of strength, resilience, and survival.
But they no longer tell me who I am.

I no longer force myself to fit into places that cost me my peace.

My mind, heart, body, and spirit are aligned.

And yes, some days are still hard. But I want you to know this—honestly and without hesitation:

I have never regretted doing my work.
Not once.

I am fitly joined with who I truly am.

And I can finally say, without hesitation or apology:

Yes.

Now she fits perfectly.

And this is my hope for you—

That when you commit to yourself and do the inner work,
you too will become fitly joined
with the woman you authentically are.

Because healing is possible.

Freedom is possible.

And the life you were meant to live—the strong, whole,
unstoppable life within you—
is still waiting for you.

And when you choose yourself,
do the work,
and refuse to give up...

One day you will look at the woman you have become and say:

Yes.

Now she fits perfectly too.

Carried By Grace

Before I close,
I want to give gratitude to the One
who made my healing possible.

Because none of this happened by my strength alone.

I was led, protected, and carried
by God every step of the way.

I didn't find this strength through willpower.
I didn't move forward because I was fearless.
And I didn't heal because I figured everything out.

I healed because God met me
right where I was —

exhausted,
uncertain,
and afraid.

When I couldn't see the way forward,
HE guided me.

When I felt exposed and vulnerable,
HE protected me.

When I cried and thought I could not go on,
HE carried me.

For me, that grace came through my relationship with Jesus.

And I will always be grateful.

All the glory belongs to HIM.

Thank you, Jesus.

About the Author

Rosita Perez

Helping women heal, reclaim identity, and step into unstoppable purpose.

Rosita Perez is a mindset coach, speaker, and author who helps women move from silently surviving to confidently thriving—because she once lived that journey herself.

After years of carrying heartbreak, painful relationships, and the pressure of being everything for everyone, Rosita discovered that real transformation begins when a woman reconnects with her true identity and the faith that anchors her.

Through practical tools and the wisdom of her Christian faith, Rosita rebuilt her life from the inside out. Her journey inspired her book, That's It, I'm Moving! A Woman's Journey from Pain to Power, where she invites women to leave behind the emotional houses that keep them stuck—fear, shame, self-doubt, and "not enough"—and step into healing, confidence, and purpose.

With warmth, authenticity, and lived experience, Rosita meets women right where they are and walks beside them as they rise into clarity, strength, and a new future.

Your past may explain your pain, but it does not define your future.

Believe It ~ Speak It ~ BE IT!

MovingForwardForLife.com

The Choice to Move Forward

If something in these pages stirred your heart, pause for a moment and notice that.

The quiet recognition.
The courage beginning to rise.
The sense that your life may be asking for something more.

This book is only the beginning.

The breaking of a seal —
from the woman you once had to be
to the woman you are becoming.

And your journey is just beginning.

If you feel ready to move out of the old houses that once held you— the ones built from fear, pain, or expectations that were never truly yours—

then this may be your moment to step toward something new.

Freedom rarely arrives by accident.

It grows when a woman chooses to become involved in her own healing and commits to building a life that finally feels like home.

If you'd like encouragement and additional reflections as you continue moving forward, I invite you to stay connected.

Visit my website:
https://www.movingforwardforlife.com

You can also find **encouragement, videos, podcasts, and meaningful conversations** on my YouTube channel.

Join me at:
https://www.youtube.com/@unstoppablemidlife

If you feel ready for deeper support, I also offer **complimentary Clarity Calls** for women who want to pause, reflect, and talk through where they are—and where they want to go next.

Sometimes one honest conversation can bring more clarity than months of trying to figure everything out alone.

You can learn more or schedule a time through my website.

For women who want ongoing guidance, I also offer personal coaching sessions designed to help you move forward with clarity, courage, and purpose.

https://www.movingforwardforlife.com/private-coaching-sessions

Until then, keep listening to the quiet voice inside you that brought you here.

Because sometimes the most powerful moment in a woman's life is the moment she realizes:

I do not have to stay where I have been.

I have the power of choice to move forward.

www.ingramcontent.com/pod-product-compliance
Lightning Source LLC
LaVergne TN
LVHW051327260626
842070LV00048B/989
* 9 7 8 1 9 7 1 3 4 9 7 2 5 *